Emigre

Graphic Design

into the Digital Realm

Written by Rudy VanderLans and Zuzana Licko with Mary E. Gray
ESSAY BY **Mr. Keedy**

A BYRON PREISS BOOK

VNR Van Nostrand Reinhold
NEW YORK

Copyrights etc.

Back cover copy by Peter Maloney.

Library of Congress Catalog Card Number 92-6773
ISBN 0-442-01380-9

Van Nostrand Reinhold is an International Thomson Publishing company.
ITP logo is a trademark under license.

I(T)P

Printed in Hong Kong

Van Nostrand Reinhold
115 Fifth Avenue
New York. New York 10003

International Thomson Publishing
Berkshire House 168-173
High Holborn. London WC1V 7AA
England

Thomas Nelson Australia
102 Dodds Street
South Melbourne 3205
Victoria. Australia

Nelson Canada
1120 Birchmount Road
Scarborough. Ontario
MIK 5G4. Canada

International Thomson Publishing GmbH
Köningswinterer Str. 418
53227 Bonn
Germany

International Thomson Publishing Asia
221 Henderson Bldg. №05-1
Singapore 0315

International Thomson Publishing Japan
Kyowa Building. 3F
2-2-1 Hirakawacho
Chiyoda-Ku. Tokyo 102
Japan

CP 16 15 14 13 12 11 10 9 8 7 6 5 4 3 2

Library of Congress Cataloging-in-Publication Data
VanderLans. Rudy. 1955-
     Emigre: Graphic Design into the Digital Realm /
  written by Rudy VanderLans. Zuzana Licko. and Mary E. Gray: essay by Mr. Keedy.
        p.   cm.
    ISBN 0-442-01380-9
1. Type-design—California—Berkeley—History—20th century. 2. Emigre Graphics—History. 3. Graphic arts—California—Berkeley—History—20th century. 4. Computerized typedesign—History. 5. Macintosh (Computer)—Programming—History. I. Licko. Zuzana. 1961-. II. Keedy. Jeffery. III Title.
Z253.3.V36   1993
686.22'2544—dc20   93-21597
                                         CIP

Contents:

This way

Dedication:

This book is dedicated to our families in Slovakia, Holland,
and the United States of America.

INTRODUCTION

When the Macintosh computer was introduced in 1984, graphic designers either came to hate it or to love it, if they had not already dismissed it. Their skepticism was understandable. Here was a machine promoted as the graphics computer of the future, but all it could show at the time were crude bitmapped typefaces and a few "simplistic" drawing and word-processing programs. To many professional designers, this computer represented a step backward. The quality standards in type and image creation had reached a level way beyond what the Macintosh offered.

Despite this criticism, the Macintosh was readily adopted by another group of so-called desktop publishers. These users were not professional graphic designers, but rather secretaries, office workers, and students. They appreciated that this computer could handle a broad range of tasks. It helped them create their flyers, newsletters, school papers, and other in-house documents quickly and cheaply. They had none of the preconceptions about the quality of type and image making that kept professional designers from buying the Macintosh. Their uninhibited use of multiple typefaces and Macintosh "gimmicks" such as outlining or shadowing fonts was considered extremely ugly by many professional graphic designers, who believed that the Macintosh would contribute to the degradation of graphic design.

Professional graphic designers first came to appreciate the Macintosh through the work of a small group of pioneering designers who were intrigued by this computer. From the very beginning, these designers saw the Macintosh's limitations as a new challenge. They not only recognized that this computer could eventually be used to copy what had been done before; they also derived inspiration from its initial crudeness. The most influential and prolific were illustrator John Hersey and graphic designer April Greiman. Hersey's witty illustration style overshadowed the crude jaggies and made people accept and look beyond the medium. Greiman, an established designer with an international reputation, included the Macintosh's low-resolution textures in her experimental work and was able to show people how the Macintosh could be used creatively. These two artists more or less paved the way for a third pioneer, Emigre Graphics, a California-based design studio founded by Rudy VanderLans and Zuzana Licko. Emigre became best known for publishing *Emigre* magazine, an experimental graphic-design journal, and Emigre Fonts, an impressive line of original typefaces for use on the Macintosh.

Working out of a simple workspace in the industrial part of West Berkeley, north of Silicon Valley, Emigre embraced the new digital medium. For them, the computer soon became much more than just a design or production tool. "FROM THAT POINT ON, GRAPHIC DESIGN WAS NEVER THE SAME FOR US." Emigre states, "ALTHOUGH IT WAS A PRIMITIVE TOOL DURING THOSE FIRST YEARS, THIS COMPUTER MADE MANY NEW THINGS POSSIBLE. WE HAD ALREADY PRINTED THE FIRST ISSUES OF *EMIGRE* MAGAZINE, BUT IT WAS THE MACINTOSH THAT MADE IT ECONOMICALLY POSSIBLE TO CONTINUE PUBLISHING. IT ALSO INSPIRED US TO DESIGN AND MANUFACTURE ORIGINAL TYPEFACES, AN AREA PREVIOUSLY DOMINATED BY ONLY A FEW LARGE TYPE FOUNDRIES." However, due to the new technology,

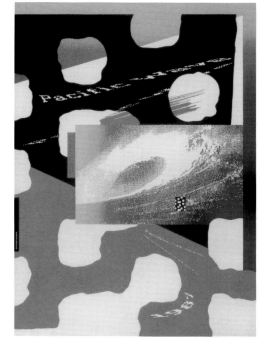

Poster, Fortuny Museum, Venice, "Pacific Wave" exhibition. **1987.**

Designed by April Greiman.

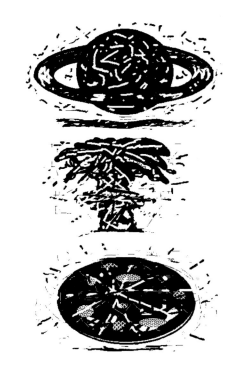

Macintosh illustration, "Planet, Bomb, Pizza." **1985.**

Illustration by John Hersey.

VanderLans and Licko felt a need to redefine their ideologies. Instead of forcing established standards to fit the computer, Emigre decided to seek new standards derived from the computer itself.

Although their layouts and type designs have garnered much attention, the strength of their work lies not in the design alone, but in the way that they have combined type design, writing, graphic design, and publishing into one, much like it was done before the days when movable type was first invented by Johann Gutenberg in 1476.

In an article titled "The New Primitives," written for *I.D.* in 1988, Emigre states: "MUCH OF THE SKEPTICISM AND DISFAVOR CURRENTLY ATTACHED TO DIGITAL IMAGES WILL DISAPPEAR AS A NEW GENERATION OF DESIGNERS ENTERS THE PROFESSION. HAVING GROWN UP WITH COMPUTERS AT HOME AND SCHOOL, THESE DESIGNERS WILL ASSIMILATE COMPUTER TECHNOLOGY INTO THE VISUAL COMMUNICATION PROCESS AS IT PENETRATES EVERYDAY PRACTICES. WITH COMPUTERS, DESIGNERS WILL BE ABLE TO PERSONALLY CONTROL THEIR WORK TO AN UNPRECEDENTED DEGREE, FROM DESIGNING CUSTOM TYPEFACES TO EDITING COLOR SEPARATIONS. THIS WILL SURELY INCREASE THE SPECIALIZATION OF THE PROFESSION. BUT IT WILL, ABOVE ALL, EXTEND THE CREATIVE PROCESS INTO PREVIOUSLY UNEXPLORED AREAS."

Rudy VanderLans and Zuzana Licko, Berkeley, Calif. **1991.**
Self-portrait.

The Macintosh grew up fast, and after nine years, it has indeed become the sophisticated graphics computer it promised to be. It is now obvious to almost everyone that the Macintosh is a powerful tool, permanently positioned within the graphic design industry.

Compiled in this book are many of the experiments, ideologies, designs and their commercial implementation, that Emigre produced while graphic design was entering the digital realm.

Storage room, Berkeley office, 1987.

Acknowledgments

Acknowledgment is due to Byron Preiss, whose personal enjoyment of our work somehow enabled him to put up with our never-ending demands for nearly three years, which is how long it took to finish this book. Without Byron Preiss, and his limitless patience, this book would have never been produced. We are also indebted to Van Nostrand Reinhold, our publisher, who, to our utter surprise, accepted virtually everything we submitted without making changes. Had we known this beforehand, this book would have looked quite different.

All kidding aside, we are very proud to say that this is our book. From the title, to the design of the pages, to the choice of typeface for the copyright notice. If there is anything that you don't like about this book, there is only one party to blame — us. And we count on you to let us know what you think. We're also deeply grateful to all the artists, graphic designers, and writers who have contributed to *Emigre* magazine over the past years. There are simply too many names to list here, but most are mentioned or have their work shown throughout this book.

A very special thank you should also go to Alice Polesky who has been *Emigre*'s copy editor and language coach since the very first issue. Since English is our second language, her guidance and input has been invaluable. It was Alice who taught us how to get right to the essence of what we tried to communicate in *Emigre* magazine. She always graciously remained in the background, satisfied by helping to verbalize our often convoluted ideas. In the process, she made us realize that language can be as powerful a tool to a graphic designer as graphic design itself.

Last but not least, we would like to thank Menno Meyjes and Marc Susan, from whom we inherited *Emigre* magazine, which was founded on the notion that you should always pursue your dreams.

Zuzana Licko & Rudy VanderLans (Emigre)

GRAPHIC DESIGNERS PROBABLY WON'T READ THIS...
but,

By Mr. Keedy

How do you write about a magazine that has had a tremendous impact on graphic design, but very few graphic designers have actually read it? When designers ask if you have seen the latest issue of *Emigre*, that's exactly what they mean, have you *seen* it. When asked if they have read *Emigre*, the response is usually "I HAVEN'T HAD TIME TO GET TO IT YET." (How long does it take?) or "IT'S TOO HARD TO READ" —a curious excuse coming from someone that is presumably "visually literate."

The illiterate graphic designer has become an unfortunate stereotype (like wearing all black and being overworked and undervalued [stop whining]). I don't think it's true that designers don't read, it's just that they don't read about design. Most design essays stink (I hope this is an exception). Design essays are usually written by some hack who wrote about lawn care products last week, or designers who haven't worked in so many years that they can't remember where they put their waxers, press-type, and T-squares.

Emigre is written for, by, and about graphic designers, like a mirror that presents designers in their own words, "warts and all." Unlike most design magazines with slick production values that frame designers in glamorous and uncritical fashion, *Emigre* has never had the luxury of beautifully printed, full-color reproductions and professional journalists and editors. What the magazine lacks in refinement, it makes up for in being relevant. This is due to Rudy VanderLans's genuine passion for new and interesting developments in design.

Rudy's point of view is not the only factor in the editorial and curatorial bias of the magazine. There are whole issues and many sections of the magazine that are determined by a guest editor/designer. This guarantees that the design and content fully embrace the subject. Rudy often functions as an editor/art director, carefully orchestrating the talents of many different designers (why don't other design magazines try this?). Speaking as one of the many contributors to *Emigre*, I think it's Rudy's contagious enthusiasm for others that compels one to go beyond pure egoism and try to do something of relevance for your fellow *Emigre* ~~readers~~ lookers.

Past contributors have been from America, Great Britain, Holland, Switzerland, and Germany and have included design schools and educators (something American design magazines have little interest in). Most of the contributors are not "rebellious kids" right out of design school but are more typically midcareer professionals struggling to sustain an interesting practice. Critics and proponents of *Emigre* often cite the "wildness" or lack of restraint in the magazine, but *Emigre* only appears "wild" in the context of the mostly vapid design magazines that preceded it. The exaggerated claims of "wildness" marginalize its important role as an outlet for exciting new ideas, ideas that are routinely ignored or completely misunderstood by the mainstream design press. The fact is, the most original ideas and intelligent work in graphic design today first appear in *Emigre*.

One thing that most clearly established *Emigre* as an "original" was its typefaces. New computer software like Fontographer made it possible for anyone (with a lot of time and patience) to create a typeface. Zuzana Licko, Rudy's wife and partner, designed typefaces like Oakland, Modula, and Matrix that put Emigre at the forefront of the new "independent" font companies. At a time when most type designers were put off by the limitations of the computer and its inability to exactly replicate existing technology, Zuzana was intrigued and inspired by the digital environment, working within limitations as if they were assets.

Because her early bitmapped fonts were of low resolution, and Zuzana likes to design within very strict parameters, her work could be misread as simplistic or crude. Zuzana's typefaces are, on close inspection, anything but crude. Whether she is working within strict confines of technically inspired forms, like Modula, Citizen, or Matrix, or within an equally restrictive conceptual framework like Totally Gothic or Journal, Zuzana's mastery of a limited palette is quite elegant. To consider Zuzana Licko's type design as crude or illegible (non-functional), weird or radical, would be incredibly shortsighted and historically ignorant. Her preference for reductivist strategies in form and her expressions of form that follows the functioning of the computer, put her in the catagory of "classic modernist," not radical reactionary.

There have been so many different and conflicting opinions expressed in *Emigre* that if you think the work is homogeneous you are not looking very closely or reading at all. There are some common concerns, characteristics, and even weaknesses that some of the *Emigre* contributors share, but to lump them all into one "style" is overly simplistic and superficial.

Graphic designers are the "scouts" of visual culture, looking ahead of the rest of the pack. Eventually "scouting" can wear you out. That's why some designers collapse into a "timeless" stasis or retreat back into nostalgia. In this state of exhaustion, we often oversimplify or overlook the obvious. In my varied career as a designer, I have been labeled as working in the "New Wave, Cranbrook, Deconstructivist, Computer, Emigre, and CalArts," styles. I don't object to the labeling and categorizing; a vocabulary has to be established to have a meaningful dialogue. What I don't like is the lack of critical criteria or context for these "styles" to be discussed with any validity. What you get instead is an uninformed opinion — "I DON'T KNOW MUCH ABOUT *THAT* KIND OF DESIGN (because i don't bother to read or find out), BUT I KNOW WHAT I LIKE, AND I DON'T LIKE *THAT*."

It is significant that *Emigre* magazine is not located in New York City, which has always had a stranglehold on the design press in America. Much of the redundancy and provincialism in design magazines in America is due to the fact that they are all geographically and ideologically located in New York's modernist dogma. Since the émigrés from Europe first came to New York and started dictating their modernist ideology to America, New York has proclaimed itself the center of American design. The very idea of a "design capital" is even more antiquated than an "art capital" in these postindustrial, postmodern times. There have been several efforts on the part of "the powers that be," or perhaps it would be more accurate to say "the powers that were," to belittle the little magazine with big ideas. Time marches on; their time is past. *Emigre*'s time is now.

Located on the "other coast" *Emigre* looks outward and forward, a magazine that ignores boundaries, while others vainly try to claim territory. Founded in Berkeley and later moved to Sacramento, *Emigre* is more an attitude than the product of a place and could have been located anywhere (except New York).

Although Rudy is by nature an "outsider" or émigré himself (emigrating to the U.S. in 1981 from Holland), he has never been actively involved in any of the many design organizations (he even declined an opportunity to join Alliance Graphique Internationale). However, through his magazine, he has established a sizable network of dedicated individuals with diverse ideologies.

Emigre is the only truly progressive and pluralistic graphic design magazine that is a locus for a decentralized discourse on design. It is an international meeting place for people interested in exploring and expanding the borders of design practice and theory. The only prerequisite is an interest in new design and an open mind. Intolerance for different ideas is the biggest obstacle in these proscribed and dogmatic times. With the mind-numbingly dull 1970s and 80s behind us, designers are waking up and starting the next millennium. *Emigre* is documenting where graphic design is going. And it's *going* to be interesting.

Over the past ten years, the work of Emigre has constantly changed as a direct result of the rapid development of the Macintosh computer. By presenting Emigre's work and ideas chronologically in this book, the authors show how the revolutionary technological changes that have taken place have affected (and will continue to affect) the creation of all kinds of graphic design. Emigre was able, through the magazine and catalogs they published and the various lectures they presented, to document many of their discoveries and experiments. Most of the quotes published throughout this book were taken from those sources.

Start.

1955–83

ludy VanderLans was born in The Hague, Holland in
955. From 1974 through 1979 he attended the Royal
Academy of Fine Art in The Hague, where he received a
Jiploma in graphic design. Although he had wanted to be-
ome an illustrator, the Academy did not offer a specific
curriculum for this. Instead VanderLans chose to study in
the graphic design department, which offered classes in
life drawing and illustration.

Without realizing what exactly he was getting involved
in, he was soon introduced to graphic design. The curriculum was a pragmatic, hands-on approach to graphic
design, modeled after the functionalist ideologies of the
International Style. There was great emphasis put on the
importance of the grid and clarity of the message. Also,
through hours of practicing calligraphy, a thorough understanding and appreciation of the history of type was
developed under the guidance of type designer Gerrit
Noordzij, who would become a decisive influence on a
group of contemporary Dutch type designers such as Just
van Rossum and Erik van Blokland.

During classes teachers often showed and discussed the
work of the leading graphic designers of the time such as
Wim Crouwel of Total Design, and Gert Dumbar of Tel Design, whose work was considered exemplary graphic design. Both these studios, in terms of design philosophy,
were exponents of a revolution that had started 60 years
earlier with El Lissitzky, the Bauhaus, De Stijl, Jan Tschichold, and Emil Ruder, to name but a few. The aims were
always simplicity and clarity and a necessity of fitting design to modern printing methods (i.e. "functionalism")
and of making design "modern," in harmony with the new
modern world being created around them.

Although intrigued by the idea of design as primarily
functionalist, VanderLans was also deeply affected by seeing the work of more expressive graphic designers whose
work did not exactly fall within these rational parameters. While at the Academy, VanderLans first en-
countered the work of Milton Glaser, whose book *Milton
Glaser Graphic Design* had just been published. The work
of this American graphic designer made a deep impression on him. It was also during this time that VanderLans
first saw copies of *U&lc*, then art directed by Herb Lubalin. Another major influence was the German designer
Heinz Edelmann. Edelmann had come to lecture at the
Academy and presented the posters he had designed for
the Westdeutscher Rundfunk. Both Glaser and Edelmann
used illustration as the primary means of communication
and used type without any of the functionalist preconceptions, whereas Lubalin turned type into illustration. They dismissed the limiting ideas of such purists as
Emil Ruder and instead argued, as Glaser put it, "THERE IS
NO SINGLE VOICE CAPABLE OF EXPRESSING EVERY IDEA, ROMANCE IS
STILL NECESSARY, ORNAMENT IS NECESSARY, AND SIMPLIFICATION
IS NOT BETTER THAN COMPLEXITY." VanderLans recognized in

Letterhead, Dutch Basketball Association. **1979.**

Designed as part of VanderLans's thesis project.

Diploma, Dutch Basketball Association. **1979.**

Designed as part of VanderLans's thesis project.

Perfect?

*"All along, starting with my design education, I was taught to believe that design was like a
science. I attended art school in Holland during the mid-seventies, and graphic design was
taught as three separate disciplines: type design, typography and design, or better yet,
problem-solving. The atmosphere and the teaching methods at the time were styled after the
Swiss, or International Style. The great thing about Swiss design, of course, is that it's
straightforward to teach and learn, because it is based on a set of rules. But it also led me
to believe that design is very exact. It was about perfect line lengths and perfect word
spacing and perfect typefaces. After graduating, we were ready to clean up the world."*
(Rudy V.)

Page spread from the 1977 Yearbook of the Royal Academy
of Fine Art, The Hague. **1977.**

Designed by Reynoud Homan and Rudy VanderLans.

the vitality and dynamism of these designers something that touched the core of his interest and ambitions.

In order to graduate, VanderLans had to first work as an apprentice. His first job, a three-month apprenticeship at Total Design in Amsterdam, was a valuable introduction to the practical implementation of form-follows-function design. Total Design, at the time, was one of the largest and most prominent design studios in the country, led by graphic designer Wim Crouwel. A straight-line descendant of early Modernist ideals, Crouwel exemplified "form follows function" when he wrote: "WE ARE BEING INUNDATED BY PRINTED TEXTS, WHICH WILL INCREASE FROM DAY TO DAY; THE TASK OF THE TYPOGRAPHIC DESIGNER IS TO ARRANGE THE TEXT IN AN ORDINARY WAY. THUS, HE WILL TRULY BE ABLE TO WORK FUNCTIONALLY. IF HE DOES NOT DO SO, HE WILL REMAIN THE ISOLATED ARTIST WHO DESIGNS 'BEAUTIFUL' TYPOGRAPHY. THE LATTER WORKS FOR A SMALL GROUP OF BIBLIOPHILES, IT SEEMS MORE IMPORTANT TO ME TO CONTRIBUTE IN A POSITIVE WAY TO THE SIMPLIFICATION OF COMMUNICATION." Such were the prevailing graphic design ideologies in Holland.

VanderLans accepted the rules and methods that were presented to him without ever questioning their validity. The legacy from which these ideas were born seemed unshakable at the time.

After his apprenticeship, in 1980, he landed a full-time job with Vorm Vijf in The Hague, then a small studio founded by Joop Ridder and Bart de Groot, two graduates from the Academy in The Hague. Here he found an atmosphere that allowed for hands-on experience and allowed VanderLans a look behind the scenes to witness firsthand the joys and pitfalls of running a small graphic-design business. Vorm Vijf was one of a handful of studios in Holland that were working toward a less rigid interpretation of Swiss typography. The bulk of the work consisted of designing corporate identities and governmental publications. After Vorm Vijf he joined Tel Design. Here, too, the design and development of identity programs, including logos, letterheads, and three-dimensional signage systems, were the mainstay of the business. The nature of these assignments usually required a great deal of research and organization and often took months or years to complete, something VanderLans soon realized he was not very interested in.

Disappointed with the experience of graphic design as a primarily organizational discipline, VanderLans decided to take some time off to travel around the United States. While in California, in 1980, he applied for graduate studies at the University of California at Berkeley band, much to his surprise, a year later he was admitted. Between 1981 and 1983, he studied photography as a graduate student under the guidance of Professor Penny D'Haemers. It was here he met Zuzana Licko, whom he married in 1983.

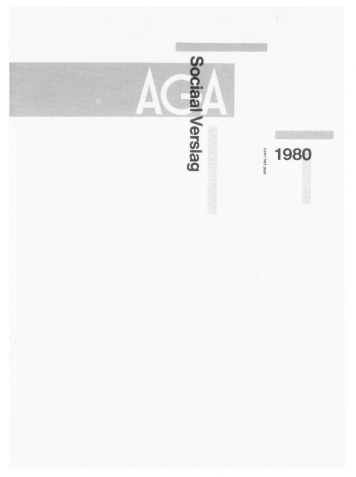

Cover annual report AGA, a gas company. **1980.**

Designed by Paul Vermijs with Rudy VanderLans at Tel Design.

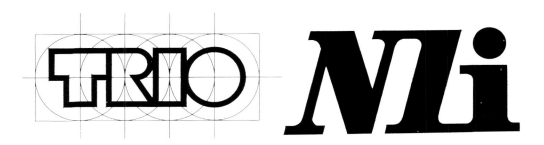

(Left) Logo for Trio, a printing company. (Right) Logo for Nordic International Leasing. **1980.**

Designed by Rudy VanderLans at Vorm Vijf.

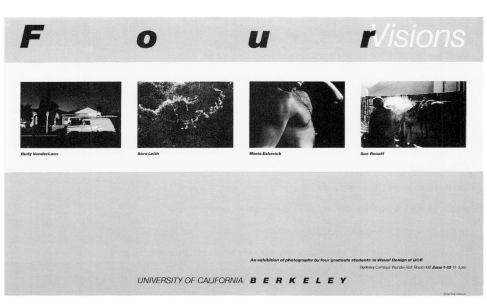

Poster, "Four Visions" exhibition. **1982.**

Designed by Rudy VanderLans while studying photography at the University of California at Berkeley.

1961–83

Zuzana Licko was born in Bratislava, Czechoslovakia, in 1961 and emigrated to the United States at the age of seven. She was first introduced to the computer at age ten playing "Space Landing," a game that required a large mainframe computer. Only five years later she was able to program the same game into a pocket calculator. While in junior college she took a computer class, where she learned to program in Pascal. It was through her father, a biomathematician at the University of California at San Francisco, that she was able to continue her involvement with computers. During the summer months she would assist him with data processing and actually designed her first typeface: a Greek alphabet that her father used in writing his scientific papers.

She entered undergraduate school at the University of California at Berkeley in 1981 to study architecture. However, after two years she decided that becoming an architect was too much like going to business school, and changed her major to visual studies. The design department at that time was being phased out and offered a loose, nondescript curriculum, allowing Licko to freely explore various directions. She took classes from designers Marc Treib, Alistair Johnston and Francis Butler, and spent hours in the library reading books on graphic design. She became interested in photography after taking courses from Penny D'Haemers and Richard Misrach. Here she experimented a great deal with various photographic printing processes, making Cibachrome color prints from color transparencies created on a color Xerox machine. Although she received grants to explore these directions and was able to occasionally exhibit the results, she also realized that photography as a fine art did not offer much security in terms of a career.

While at Berkeley, she took an entry-level computer programming class for architectural drafting, where she experimented for the first time with the design of low-resolution type. Toward the end of her studies she also took a work-study class with Aaron Marcus, whose Berkeley-based graphic-design studio was involved with the development of digital fonts.

Feeling frustrated with the lack of a focused curriculum at Berkeley, Licko was relieved when college was over and done with. There is one class in particular that she remembers: the only calligraphy class she ever took. She remembers it because, although left-handed, she was forced to write with her right hand and didn't enjoy the experience. "I'VE NEVER BEEN ATTRACTED TO DOING CALLIGRAPHY," she says, "WITH CALLIGRAPHY THERE WAS SUCH A SET WAY OF DOING THINGS THAT UNLESS YOU COULD TECHNICALLY OUT-DO THE NEXT GUY IT BECAME JUST A MATTER OF PRODUCTION. HOW MANY HOURS COULD YOU SPEND DOING THIS? THAT TO ME WAS MORE THERAPEUTIC THAN CREATIVE." Years later, as she embarked upon her career as a type designer, she realized how her

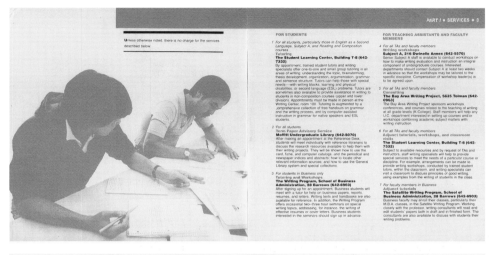

Letter press printed business card. **1982.**

Designed and printed by Zuzana Licko.

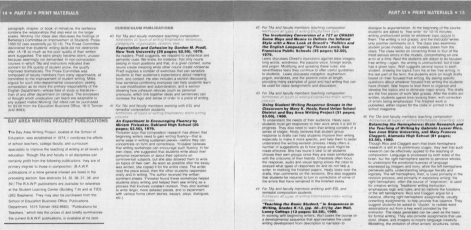

Page spreads from the catalog "Improving Students' Writing Skills" for UCB. **1983.**

Designed by Zuzana Licko.

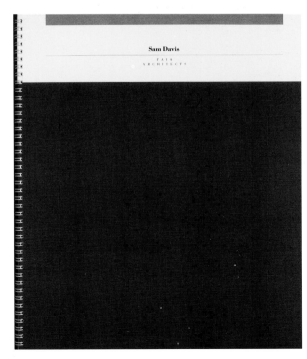

Cover of a capabilities brochure for an architect. **1984.**

Designed by Zuzana Licko.

dismissal of calligraphy contributed to her unique approach to type design, since conventional type design is firmly rooted in calligraphy. After graduating she worked a short time for graphic designer Gordon Chun in Berkeley, but soon realized that she wanted to work for herself, and started to work as a free-lance designer in 1985.

In 1983, VanderLans had landed a job at the *San Francisco Chronicle* under Art Director John Sullivan. He was involved in a variety of activities, ranging from editorial and spot illustrations to cover designs for the Sunday paper inserts to producing maps and graphs. At the newspaper, none of the sophisticated functionalist ideas about typography held up. The work required a rapid-fire design method, allowing only hours for the development of an idea and its execution. It was obviously more important to finish the work on time than to come up with solutions that were in accordance with accepted typographic norms. Besides, the rules were laid down clear and simple. Primarily run by editors, the approach to typography at the newspaper was "common sense." Although it was at first a frustrating experience, VanderLans later realized that working at the newspaper was a major learning experience. The illustrations and page layouts needed to be understood immediately by the readers and were entirely subservient to the contents. "White space," which was considered an important design ingredient in traditional typography, was now a commodity.

Postage stamp. **1987**.

Designed by Max Kisman.

(Not so) *Perfect*

"In Holland, graphic design is quite well integrated into society. Everything from postage stamps to money to telephone books is produced with a great deal of respect for design. The Dutch government is one of the largest graphic-design clients in the country. They hire the leading and most innovative studios to design their ministry logos, identities, governmental publications, etc. The entire population is exposed to these designs, which has made the Dutch a visually sophisticated audience.

Therefore, when I came to the United States in 1981 and started working at a newspaper, of all places, I was just stunned. It was so different from Holland in terms of the design climate. And I don't know about other newspapers, but the SAN FRANCISCO CHRONICLE is primarily designed and put together by editors; designers are seen as mere facilitators.

"At first this new role was difficult to accept, because all the things that they had taught me in art school about legibility and good type and bad type were swept aside. The editors had their own set of rules and you could argue with them forever about increasing line spacing, or changing type styles to increase legibility, but in the end they'd say, "Well, we have 750,000 people reading the newspaper each day and they're not complaining about these things." And this was mind-boggling at first, because it seemed to me that they were breaking every rule in the book of typography, but obviously they weren't doing badly at all. People read the newspaper every day without any problem and oftentimes under less than perfect reading conditions; in the bus, in the car, while walking to work. This is when I realized that all the rules, formulae, and form-follows-function ideas that I was carrying around in my head really were not applicable to each and every item. Some things, I came to understand, are better off left alone.

It wasn't that the editors didn't accept or respect the ideas about perfect typefaces and line lengths, it's just that they had their own idea about what they called the newspaper "look" and they were quite suspicious of sophisticated design ideas. To them, newspapers should look like newspapers. It was all done very intentionally. So I figured, if the editors could get away with an approach that defied everything I had taken for granted, maybe I could do the same, and challenge the preconceived ideas that I had about type and typography.

"How about legibility, though? If you do have to concern yourself with making things legible and understandable, why not learn from something as popular as a newspaper? "Poorly" designed daily newspapers have proved to be just as legible as some of the most rational, well organized, objective Swiss typography, mostly because people read best what they read most. If we assume that, then maybe graphic designers should style their work after the junk mail, or the newspapers or television graphics that we see on a daily basis. If we need to be concerned with legibility, we shouldn't force an aesthetic on people, like Jan Tschichold did by writing his infamous book DIE NEUE TYPOGRAPHIE or as Emil Ruder did through his teachings at Basel and the many books that he wrote; we should give people what they're already used to reading instead.

"Ultimately, the newspaper editors' ideas were all based upon simple typographic notions and a great deal of common sense. But they also assumed that everybody enjoys reading in the same way. This is where I felt that there was room for experimentation, because I think that people read in many different ways and are more sophisticated than they get credit for when it comes to taking in information. All throughout the day, people are exposed to an enormous variety of information coming to them from many different sources. Since people have learned to read certain newspapers every day, it stands to reason that they can adapt to anything. Even though I realize that the designer's primary role is to make sense out of the information that is out there, I feel a need to do this in such a way that the result can not be ignored. This sometimes means pushing at the boundaries of legibility a bit.

"When, in 1984, we started EMIGRE magazine, it quickly became the testing ground for these experiments. But the experimentation was never meant as an end in itself. We were convinced that a magazine was the perfect medium for conveying ideas and opinions to a large audience. Also, there was only a handful of other magazines that we really liked ourselves and we wanted to publish our own work. So what better reasons for starting our own magazine? We invested the fifteen hundred dollars from our savings in printing 500 copies of the first issue."

(Rudy V.)

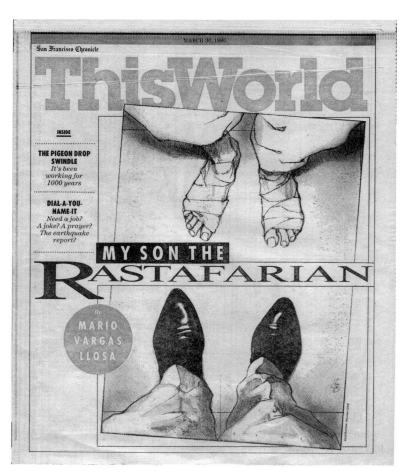

Front cover, sunday supplement, *San Francisco Chronicle*. **1986**.

Design by Rudy VanderLans. Illustration by William Cone.
Art Direction by John Sullivan.

Front cover (top half), *San Francisco Chronicle*. **1985**.

Designed by the editors.

1983 (4)

Through his involvement, in 1982, with the traveling exhibition "Dutch Artists on the West Coast," VanderLans met artist Marc Susan and screenwriter Menno Meyjes, two fellow Dutchmen who both lived in San Francisco. Discouraged with the struggle of getting their personal work published, the three opted, in 1983, to start their own magazine, which seemed a perfect vehicle to showcase their unpublished work and that of other, like-minded artists. Although the initial idea was to create a magazine devoted to Dutch immigrants living in California, it soon grew to include artists from around the world, an obvious choice for a magazine published in the multi-cultural Bay Area. The name *Emigre* was proposed by Meyjes, who imagined the magazine to be a tabloid featuring international artists and their art.

It took exactly one year for the first issue of *Emigre* to be published in 1984. Financed by VanderLans, *Emigre* 1 was printed as a limited edition of 500 copies and featured the work of artist friends ranging from architects to poets to photographers. Included in the issue was a graphic presentation of one of Meyjes's original screenplays that he had written for Francis Ford Coppola's San Francisco-based Zoëtrope studios. Also featured were various bilingual poems written by Marc Susan and laid out by VanderLans, who used enlarged versions of the actual typewritten poems together with found imagery supplied by Susan. Also in this issue are layouts of black-and-white photographs made by VanderLans during his studies at UC Berkeley. Although the original photographs were traditional black-and-white prints, VanderLans decided to significantly manipulate the prints for reproduction in *Emigre*. Instead of trying to reproduce the prints exactly, which he knew would fall short, considering the limited printing facilities he had at his disposal, he instead opted for randomly tearing his precious photographs and collaging them together to create something entirely new. This approach of working within the restrictions and utilizing the characteristics of the medium at hand would become an *Emigre* staple. All the layouts in *Emigre* 1 were created with Xeroxed imagery and typewriter type and show evidence of VanderLans's need to break with "neutral" typography and to find an alternative means of expression. The layouts were forcedly expressive, lacking a traditional grid. Not to be discounted is the fact that VanderLans had to pay the printing bill, which also had a significant effect on the way *Emigre* looked.

Pre Macintosh era, Berkeley, 1983.

Front cover, *Emigre* 1. **1984.**

Designed by Rudy VanderLans.

Beginning

"Initially, the magazine featured a rather diverse collection of work by young artists, people we admired, ranging from writers to designers to architects. Most of these people were from our immediate environment; they just presented themselves to us. There was no budget to assign specific pieces, therefore we relied on existing work. We used whatever we found in their portfolios that appealed to us, which gave the magazine a rather eclectic appearance. The only real theme for the magazine at that time was the experience of being exposed to various cultures. We wanted to create a romantic magazine about places and ideas and how living in different places could influence and change the artist's work. This is how we arrived at the name EMIGRE.*"*
(Rudy V.)

Page spread. *Emigre* 1. **1984.**

Poems by Marc Susan. Designed by Rudy VanderLans.

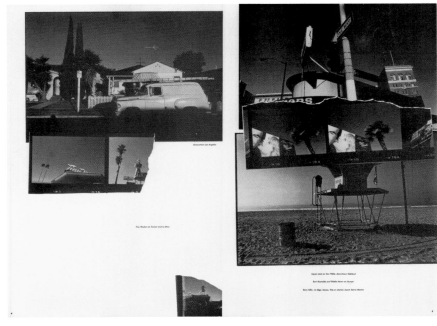

Page spread. *Emigre* 1. **1984.**

Design and photography by Rudy VanderLans.

Since there was no budget to produce *Emigre*, and since the Macintosh was not yet available, these first issues were created using primarily typewriter type and Xerox reproduction techniques. In order to make the type look less like ordinairy typewriter type, VanderLans either enlarged or reduced the texts. These were then pasted onto boards together with the Xeroxed images.

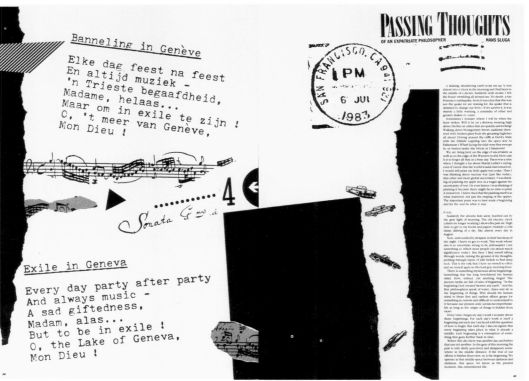

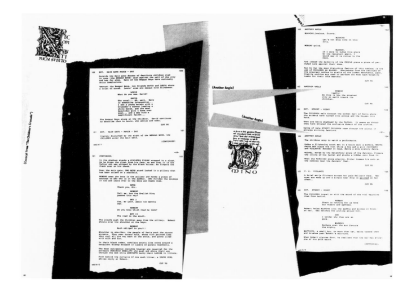

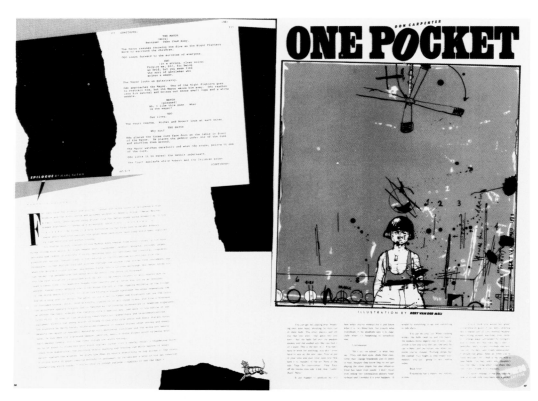

4 Page spreads, *Emigre* 1. **1984.**

Designed by Rudy VanderLans.

Painting, "Immigrant X," *Emigre* 1. **1984.**

Illustration by John Hersey.

Emigre. **The magazine that ignores boundaries.**

(the concept)

"The focus of *Emigre* is on the unique perspective of contemporary poets, writers, journalists, graphic designers, photographers, architects, and artists who live or have lived outside their native countries. Their influence on culture is diverse and significant: they import it and export it; they offer new interpretations, comparisons, ideas, and a certain universal wisdom acquired through juggling conflicting values and lifestyles. Their perspective is born of the émigré spirit that all of us share but exercise to various degrees. The true émigrés seek adventuresome, romantic, and human experiences; their lives convey the feelings shared by the artist in us all, the feeling of boundaries ignored and the pursuit of dreams.

In a continuing portrait series, *Emigre* pays tribute to some of the greatest expatriates of all time: Lord Byron, Paul Gauguin, Vincent van Gogh, David Hockney, Christopher Isherwood, James Joyce, Piet Mondriaan, Vladimir Nabokov, Ezra Pound, Arthur Rimbaud, George Sand, Gertrude Stein, and others."

Excerpt from a letter sent to potential advertisers. **1984.**

Page, "Samuel Beckett," *Emigre* 3. **1985.**

Painting by Dana F. Smith.

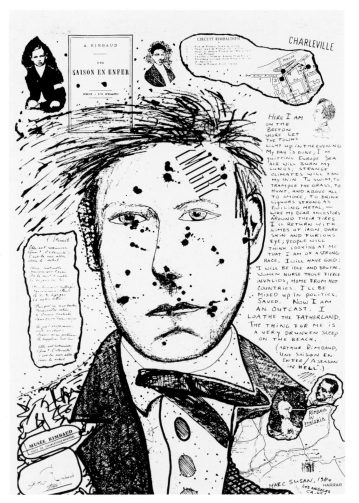

Page, "Arthur Rimbaud," *Emigre* 2. **1985.**

Collage by Marc Susan.

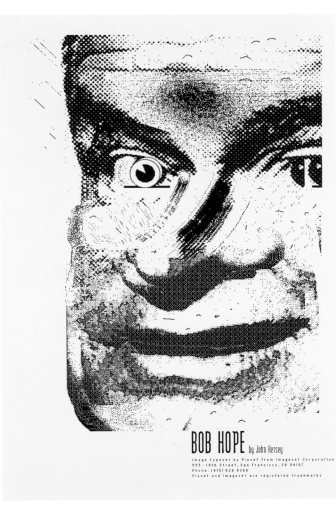

Page, "Bob Hope," *Emigre* 6. **1985.**

Illustration by John Hersey.

Page, "Vladimir Nabokov," *Emigre* 2. **1985.**

Painting by William Cone.

1 9 8 4 (5)

In 1984, as the second issue of *Emigre* was being produced, the Macintosh was released. Shortly after, *MacWorld*, a new magazine devoted to the Macintosh computer, was offering to teach a select group of illustrators how to use the Macintosh. The editors were eager to illustrate their editorials with actual Macintosh art, but had a difficult time finding editorial illustrators who liked computers. Art director Bruce Charonet, who knew VanderLans through his work for the *San Francisco Chronicle*, invited VanderLans and Licko for a trial run. Both were immediately impressed by the Macintosh's capabilities and by how easy it was to use. Two weeks later, they bought their first 128K Macintosh.

While VanderLans used it primarily to create simple MacPaint illustrations, Licko discovered its type-design possibilities. Through the Berkeley Macintosh Users Group, she came across a public-domain software called FontEditor, which allowed her to design low-resolution typefaces for use on the Macintosh screen and dot-matrix Imagewriter. This was a breakthrough of some sort. Although it has always been possible to design and draw a typeface, the actual typesetting equipment one needs to set type freely is cumbersome and highly specialized equipment, usually owned and operated by typesetters and typefoundries. The Macintosh allowed you to store the data that defines the typeface and then access it through the keyboard. Now, for the first time, it was possible for any individual to design and draw a typeface and then actually use it without restrictions.

With the Macintosh, Licko was able to continue what she had started in college. The first typefaces she created, Emperor, Emigre, and Oakland, were sporadically used in *Emigre* magazine, offering VanderLans an alternative to the typewriter type that he was forced to use since no budget for photo-typesetting existed. Licko was fascinated by the restrictions that the Macintosh presented. Having little knowledge of calligraphy and therefore not hindered by the traditions and conventions of type design, she instead based the designs of her typefaces upon simple concepts derived from the low-resolution characteristics of the Macintosh. Most of her fonts used modular elements with which she could create all characters.

It was not until then that she was introduced to Herbert Bayer's early experiments with modular type and Donald Knuth's MetaFont. MetaFont is a computer program, developed at Stanford University, that would make obsolete the tedious redrawing of repetitive elements in typefaces. She was also fascinated by Chuck Bigelow's writing on the subject of digital type. Interested in their work and eager to solicit a response to her typeface designs, Licko wrote letters to both Knuth and Bigelow but without reply. She also submitted her typeface designs to Letraset, but received form letters saying "Thanks, but no thanks."

The Macintosh 128K at Licko and Vanderlans's Berkeley apartment. 1985.

Puzzles

"Ever since I was first introduced to graphic design, I heard everybody say how bad digital type looked and how it was impossible to make it look any better. This really intrigued me. Whenever anybody makes a statement like that, I have difficulty agreeing. I was reading books on the history of graphic design and in the final chapter they would always mention something about digital type and show the same typefaces like OCR A or B. Some of them were actually interesting but never really good, especially for setting text. Then I read Chuck Bigelow's writings on the subject of digital type. I was fascinated and agreed with a lot of the things he was saying, but when I looked at the visual results I was a bit disappointed with how traditional his type still looked.

"So I saw that there was something unexplored and interesting there and I wanted to try my own hand at it. That's when I got involved with designing my first low-resolution type in a computer class that I took. But every time I asked for advice, people kept telling me it was really a lost cause, that it couldn't be done. So I thought that anything I would do would be better than what was out there.

"I enjoy things that are like puzzles; anything that is tremendously restrictive, where there are very few choices but you have to make it work. If I get too many choices I become overwhelmed. I just don't have the time and patience to look at every possible scenario. This is the problem I have with graphic design. I never got the feeling that I found the final solution to a problem. Although today I can more easily design a typeface like Triplex, which is a bit more traditional and less modular, than I could have five years ago, I still get most of my creative energy out of solving these puzzles. When nobody is able to make something work, I get inspired to find out what I might do with it.

"I started my venture with bitmap type designs, created for the coarse resolutions of the computer screen and dot matrix printer. The challenge was that because the early computers were so limited in what they could do you really had to design something special. Even if it was difficult to adapt calligraphy to lead and later lead to photo technology, it could be done, but it was physically impossible to adapt 8-point Goudy Old Style to 72 dots to the inch. In the end you couldn't tell Goudy Old Style from Times Roman or any other serif text face.

Later I discovered quite a bit of material that I should have seen before I started. Issue number 6 of BASELINE magazine, which was edited by Erik Spiekermann, was very informative and thought provoking. It introduced me to the work of some very important type designers. But then again, if I had read it beforehand, I might never have tried to explore the really basic ideas that I had."

(Zuzana L.)

Emperor

OAKLAND

Emigre

Digital typeface designs. 1985.

Designed by Zuzana Licko.

"A type design requires a delicate balance between repetition of elements and distinction among the various characters. Recurring forms provide unity and the overall look of the face, but no character may be so similar to another as to cause confusion between them, or so different from the rest that it appears alien within the face. Achieving this within the limited parameters of bitmap type was quite a challenge"

(Zuzana L.)

Emperor Fifteen: AaBbCcD

dEeFfGgHhIiJjKkLlMmNnOoPpQ qRrSsTtUuVvWwXxYyZz

(1 2 3 4 5 6 7 8 9 0)

Emperor Nineteen: AaBbCcDdEeFfGgH

hIiJjKkLlMmNnOoPpQqRrSsTtUuVvWwXxYyZz12 34567890

Emperor Ten: A

aBbCcDdEeFfGgHh IiJjKkLlMmNnOoPpQqRrSsTtUuVvWwXxYyZz

1 2 3 4 5 6 7 8 9 0

Emperor Eight: AaBbCcDdEe

FfGgHhIiJjKkLlMmNnO oPpQqRrSsTtUuVvWwXxYy

Zz1234567890

Digital typeface designs. Top to bottom: Emperor Nineteen, Emperor Fifteen, Emperor Ten, and Emperor Eight. **1985.**

Designed by Zuzana Licko.

PRICE FIVE$

PUBLISHERS
Marc Susan SENIOR EDITOR
Rudy VanderLans ART DIRECTOR, DESIGNER
Zuzana Licko ASSISTANT DESIGNER

ASSOCIATE EDITORS
Menno Meyjes
Alice Polesky
Hans Sluga
Andrei Toluzakov

ASSISTANT EDITORS
Karen Keenan
Anne Telford

SPECIAL THANKS TO
Tom Bonauro
Gordon Chun
Calvin Ahlgren
Svetlana Darsalia
Gai T. Gherardi
Charlotte Gusay
Ron Chan

EMIGRE IS PUBLISHED ABOUT TWICE A YEAR BY EMIGRE GRAPHICS.
COPYRIGHT 1985 BY EMIGRE GRAPHICS. ALL RIGHTS RESERVED. NO PART OF THIS PUBLICATION MAY BE REPRODUCED WITHOUT WRITTEN PERMISSION FROM THE ARTISTS OR EMIGRE GRAPHICS.

EMIGRE

A LIMITED NUMBER OF EMIGRE COPIES ARE STILL AVAILABLE. SEND FIVE DOLLARS PLUS POSTAGE (1.50 TO U.S. AND CANADA) (2.00 TO EUROPE) TO EMIGRE GRAPHICS POST OFFICE BOX 175 46 SHATTUCK SQUARE BERKELEY CA 94704-1069

Contents page, *Emigre* 2. First use of Zuzana Licko's bitmap fonts Emigre and Oakland. **1985.**

Designed by Rudy VanderLans.

EMPEROR 8
EMPEROR 10
EMPEROR 15
EMPEROR 19

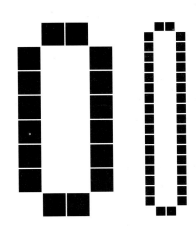

The Emperor, Universal, Oakland, and Emigre faces were originally designed as bitmap fonts for use on the 72-dot-per-inch computer screen and dot-matrix printer before high-resolution outline fonts were available. Since the coarse resolution does not allow for a faithful representation of the same design for a variety of sizes, these faces relate by a system of whole pixel increments. The Emperor family consists of a series of faces that maintain the same one-pixel stem to two-pixel counter ratio, while varying the vertical cap height. The Universal family uses a one-pixel stem to three-pixel counter ratio, and Oakland and Emigre families use a two-pixel stem to two-pixel counter ratio.

Scaling Emperor Eight (left "O") and Emperor Fifteen (right "O") to the same capital height measure illustrates why a higher resolution is required to render Emperor Fifteen.

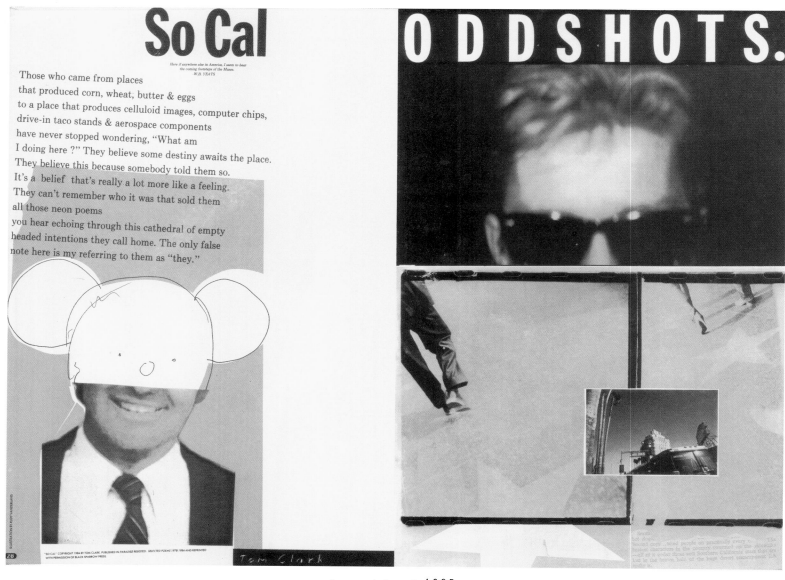

Page spread. *Emigre* 2. **1 9 8 5.**

Design and photography by Rudy VanderLans.

Page spread. *Emigre* 2. **1 9 8 5.**

Designed by Rudy VanderLans. Illustration (right) by Diane Best.

Page spread. *Emigre* 2. **1 9 8 5.**

Designed by Rudy VanderLans. Illustration (right) by Tom Bonauro.

Page spread. *Emigre* 2. **1 9 8 5.**

Designed by Rudy VanderLans. Woodcut (left) by Carlos Llerena Aguirre.

OAKLAND SIX:

ABCDEFGHIJKLMNO P Q R S T U

V W X Y Z 1234567890

Oakland Eight: AaBbCcDd &

EeFfGgHhIiJjKkLlMmNnOoPpQqRr SsTtUu

VvWwXxYyZz (1 2 3 4 5 6 7 8 9 0)

Oakland Ten: AaBbCcDdEeFfGgH

hIiJjKkLlMmNnOoPpQqRrSsTtUuV

vWwXxYyZz1234567890

Oakland Fifteen:

AaBbCcDdEeF ƒ G g HhIiJjKkLlMmNnOoPpQqRrSs

TtUuVvWwXxYyZz/ * 1234567890

Bitmap typeface designs. Top to bottom: Oakland Six,
Oakland Eight, Oakland Ten and Oakland Fifteen. **1985.**

Designed by Zuzana Licko.

(415) 841 4161
Emigre Graphics
48 Shattuck Square
Box 175
Berkeley, CA 94704-1140

Business card, Emigre Graphics. **1985.**

Designed by Rudy VanderLans.

Poster announcing a lecture by Rudy VanderLans at the Alberta
College of Art using Oakland as the primary typeface. **1989.**

Designed by Rudy VanderLans.

OAKLAND 6
OAKLAND 8
OAKLAND 10
OAKLAND 15

The coarser the resolution, the more limited is the possibility of pixel placement, and the variety of
representable font characteristics is limited accordingly. Emperor Eight and Oakland Six are two designs
that use the minimum number of pixels needed to define a complete alphabet; the numbers, Eight and Six
refer to the number of pixels that compose the capital height.

UNIVERSAL NINETEEN:abc

defghijklmnopqrstuvwxyz [1234567890]

UNIVERSAL EIGHT:Aa

BbCcDdEeFfGgHhIiJjKkLlMmNnOoPpQ qRr

SsTtUuVvWwXxYyZz

Bitmap typeface designs. Top to bottom: Universal Eight and
Universal Nineteen. **1985.**

Designed by Zuzana Licko.

[123456 7890]

Cover, Digital Fonts booklet. **1985.**

Designed by Zuzana Licko.

Inspiration

"For centuries the design of typefaces has existed as an exclusive discipline reserved for specialists; today the personal computer provides the opportunity to create customized alphabets with an increased potential for personalization and expression. The design and manufacture of fonts can now be integrated into a single medium, allowing for a more interactive design approach.

"The first typographers originated from the printing profession, where they controlled virtually all stages of design and production. Later, with the advent of photo technology, type design, graphic design and printing grew into specialized fields. On the electronic page, text and image are once again created simultaneously with the same medium, bringing back greater control. Traditionally, the printing of type involved duplicating the letterforms from wood, metal, or photographic masters by a derivative process. This copying degraded the quality of image with each reproduction step.

"The digital letterform, however, does not exist in a physical master form. Instead, the digital printer generates each letter as an original, yielding an image that is perfectly accurate and consistent. The quality of the letters is now dependent solely on the resolution of the output device.

"Digital technology has advanced the state of graphic art by a quantum leap into the future, thereby turning designers back to the most primitive of graphic ideas. Integrating design and production, the computer has reintroduced craft as the source of inspiration.

"Because the computer is an unfamiliar medium, designers must reconsider many basic rules previously taken for granted. This has brought excitement and creativity to aspects of design that have been forgotten since the days of letterpress. With computers, many alternatives can be quickly and economically reviewed, which dramatically changes the design process. Although the speed of computerized production does not necessarily result in a faster turnout of successful designs, it does enable the artist to spend more time evaluating the options. Today's designers must learn to discriminate intelligently among all of the choices, a task requiring a thorough understanding of fundamentals.

The adaptation of our alphabet to today's digital technology is re-evaluating the traditions in which today's letterforms are still deeply rooted. The new access to type design and manufacture has created an opportunity for a new breed of type designer; free of traditional preconceptions.

"Just as the need for additional type designs was being questioned, the computer opened up a fresh challenge. It is impossible to transfer typefaces between technologies without alterations because each medium has its peculiar qualities and thus requires unique designs."
(Zuzana L.)

"In terms of design, our direction became more focused when we started using the Macintosh. Besides the fact that the Macintosh made publishing our magazine affordable, it also made our typesetting bills almost negligible while, simultaneously, we gained tremendous control over the output of type. We were able to experiment endlessly without having to go through a hired typesetter. It was especially exciting to sit behind this machine right at the beginning, when no one else had really explored it yet. There were no visual standards and no existing language to copy or be inspired by. And it was during this first year that we developed most of our visual vocabulary and ideas about how we wanted to design. For instance, Zuzana's early PostScript typefaces are derived from the low-resolution typefaces that she had created for screen display and dot-matrix printing."
(Rudy V.)

Emigre Fifteen: AaBb C c D d E e F f G g H h
I i J j K k L l M m N n O o P p Q q R r S s T t U u V v W w X
x Y y Z z (1234567890)

Emigre Fourteen: [A a B b C c d]
E e F f G g H h I i J j K k L l M m N n O o P p Q q
R r S s T t U u V v W w X x Y y Z z
(1 2 3 4 5 6 7 8 9 0)

Emigre Ten: A a B b C c D d E e F f G g
H h I i J j K k L l M m N n O o P p Q q R r S s T t
U u V v W w X x Y y Z z] (1234567890)

Emigre Eight: A a B b C c D d E e
F f G g H h I i J j K k L l M m N n O o P p Q q R r S s T t U u V v W w X x Y y Z z 1 2 3 4 5 6
(7 8 9 0)

Digital typeface designs. Top to bottom: Emigre Fifteen,
Emigre Fourteen, Emigre Ten and Emigre Eight. 1985.
Designed by Zuzana Licko.

and in this and many other cultures there is always a fascination with talent dying young. ⧉ ISN'T IT DECADENT TO DWELL ON THAT? ⧉ Of course it's decadent! It's like singing "I hope I die before I get old". But when you get old, you don't want to die at all! You want to be a wily old guy singing "My Way" and being paid handsomely for it. ⧉ DID MARLOWE CHOOSE THE COURSE OF HIS LIFE, MORALLY SPEAKING? ⧉ The devil is here to test our free will. If there was no devil, man would never have a moral choice, he would simply be *good*, because there would be no other choice to make. Marlowe

ABOUT sincere! YOUR W nature. Institute realized I don't Also, my people. director not sitti

Detail (real size) of a section from an article published in *Emigre* 3, which was typeset on the Macintosh and printed out on the ImageWriter using the bitmap fonts Emigre Fourteen and Oakland Six.

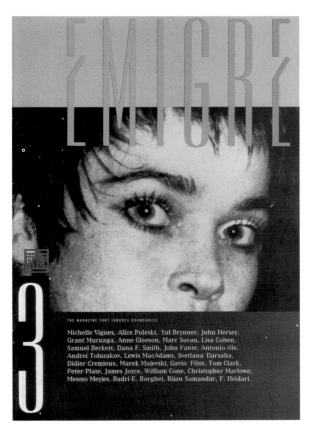

Cover, *Emigre* 3. **1985.**

Designed by Rudy VanderLans.

Page spread, *Emigre* 3. **1985.**

Designed by Rudy VanderLans.

Emigre 3 was the first issue in which all early,
coarse-resolution, Emigre
fonts were used through-
out. The texts were set
using either MacWrite or
MacPaint and were print-
ed out in galleys on the
ImageWriter, a low-
resolution (72 dpi) out-
put device — PostScript
and the LaserWriter
were not yet available.
The galleys were then re-
duced on the stat camera
in order to make the
coarse resolution of the
typefaces less noticeable.

Page spread, *Emigre* 3. **1985.**

Designed by Rudy VanderLans. Illustration by John Hersey.

1986 (7)

In 1986 VanderLans started working only part-time at the *San Francisco Chronicle*, allowing him to spend more time to work on *Emigre* and free-lance work. Together with Licko they rented a small studio space in West Berkeley and started doing free-lance illustration and design work. Most of the work consisted of illustrations for Apple Computer and the various computer magazines that were being started as the graphic computer revolution was in full swing. They also worked on the design of *Mac-Week*, a new weekly magazine started by Michael Tsjong. *MacWeek* was to be entirely created on the Macintosh and VanderLans helped to create the basic design for the first issues with the use of bug-ridden beta versions of various page makeup programs.

Cover and inside page design proposal for *MacWeek*. **1987.**

Designed by Rudy VanderLans.

APPLE LAUNCHES NEW ASSAULT ON CORPORATE BASTIONS

Previous efforts by Apple to get the Macintosh accepted in the corporate world have been frustrated by the strong presence of IBM, but a new low-key approach may be bearing fruit.

BY ELIZABETH RANNEY

Illustration for *Info World* magazine. **1986.**

Art directed by Jeff Berlin. Created by Rudy VanderLans.

Illustration for *MacWorld* magazine. **1986.**

Art directed by Bruce Charonet. Created by Rudy VanderLans.

Illustration

"We were introduced to the Macintosh when MACWORLD *magazine invited a group of illustrators to try out the new machine. They were eager to teach illustrators to use the Mac to create editorial illustrations for* MACWORLD *magazine. The minute Zuzana and I sat behind the Mac, we knew that this machine was made for us. For about a year, I became preoccupied with computer illustrations. And these Macintosh illustrations were in demand! This was an entirely new market and there were only a few illustrators who actually enjoyed working on the Mac. Most of the money we earned doing this was used to pay for the printing of the early issues of* EMIGRE.*

(Rudy V.)

Video camera hooked up to Macintosh to capture images for use in illustrations, Berkeley office, 1986.

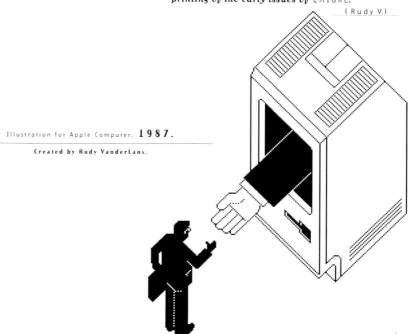

Illustration for Apple Computer. **1987.**

Created by Rudy VanderLans.

The exhibition "Dutch Artists on the West Coast" held in 1982 had also introduced VanderLans to Henk Elenga, one of the founding members of Hard Werken, a Dutch design collective. Elenga had moved to Hollywood to open the "L.A. Desk," the U.S. office for the Hard Werken group, and his work had a profound influence on VanderLans. In the late seventies and early eighties, Hard Werken had broken away from the dominant Swiss functionalist tradition that existed in Holland. Together with a few other designers, they were instrumental in changing the face of Dutch graphic design. As a collective they had initially been responsible for the design and publication of a cultural magazine called *Hard Werken*. Many of the members of the Hard Werken collective, including Elenga, were educated in the fine arts, not graphic design, and VanderLans was fascinated by their non-traditionalist attitude to design. "WE ARE NOT CONCERNED WITH FUNCTIONALITY OR LEGIBILITY," said Hard Werken, "BUT RATHER WITH THE TOTAL PICTURE, EVEN IF THAT PICTURE IS ILLEGIBLE AT TIMES." VanderLans tried to incorporate the intuitive and expressive Hard Werken approach in his own work, which was still heavily influenced by the structured typography taught at the Academy. Early copies of *Emigre* magazine show similarities to Hard Werken's magazine in terms of size, contents, and design, and articles and interviews with Hard Werken as well as Elenga's graphic and furniture designs appeared in early issues of *Emigre*.

VanderLans was also inspired by Elenga's interdisciplinary skills and by his efforts to produce and market his own products. The prototypes of the lamps and tables that Elenga designed he manufactured himself in the back of his studio on Melrose Avenue. Elenga also designed the flyers that advertised his furniture designs, creating a consistent visual appearance for all his products. Elenga's entrepreneurial spirit inspired VanderLans and encouraged him to believe that it was possible for one person to design, manufacture, and sell products.

Cover, *Hard Werken* magazine. **1981.**

Designed by Hard Werken.

Entrepreneurs

"While HARD WERKEN *magazine inspired me visually, there were two other magazines that directly inspired me to try and publish my own magazine. One was* 4-TAXIS, *a magazine that was devoted to "The International Boondocks." The other was* FURORE, *a Dutch magazine published by Piet Schreuders, which was devoted largely to American culture. What I liked most about these magazines was that neither gave me the impression they were published simply as an excuse to sell advertising. The articles were always very esoteric and gave me the feeling they were written for me alone. But more importantly, each magazine was published by only one or two people, giving me the impresson that I could possibly do this alone. I was, of course, conveniently ignoring the fact that neither magazine lasted very long"*

(Rudy V.)

Page spread, *Hard Werken* magazine. **1981**

Designed by Hard Werken.

Brochure announcing "De Stam," a lighting fixture designed and produced by Elenga. **1983.**

Designed by Henk Elenga.

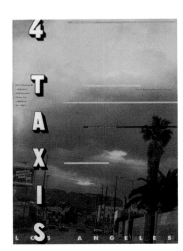

Covers of *Furore* and *4-Taxis.* **1975, 1984.**

Left: Designed by Piet Schreuders. Right: designed by 4 Taxis.

Besides the illustration work on the Macintosh for Apple Computer and a variety of computer magazines, Emigre worked mainly on low-budget projects for non-profit organizations. With minimal budgets available, great inventiveness and resourcefulness were necessary, not unlike when he designed *Emigre*. Many design jobs were created in close relationship with local printers using stock paper and one- or two-color printing. Of these printers Emigre most frequently used Lompa Printing in Albany, California.

A show of offset-printed artist books at San Francisco Camera Arts in 1985 inspired VanderLans to further explore offset printing. He applied for and received a grant to spend a month at the Visual Studies Workshop in Rochester, New York. Here he was free to play with the letterpress and offset printing. It was here, too, that he discovered the creative potential of stripping while producing his project "Positively Palmtree." Excited about the many discoveries, upon his return from Rochester he was able to talk printer Don Cushman at the West Coast Print Center into letting him strip the next issue of *Emigre*.

The issue, *Emigre* 4, is full of stripping mistakes and represents VanderLans's early experiments with layering image, type, and colors. Creating knockouts, traps, and the necessary tight registration remained difficult to do for a novice stripper. In order to solve this problem VanderLans misregistered and "overprinted" imagery and type on purpose, which often resulted in a complex-looking layered effect. Later, critics mistakenly interpreted this to be a Macintosh contribution. The intuitive, expressive qualities that VanderLans had found so seductive in Hard Werken's work he was now able to generate himself through stripping. Otherwise, his work remained highly structured and simple.

The West Coast Print Center had until then printed all issues of *Emigre* on a small 18"x 24" Heidelberg. This size press soon proved too small to print an oversize magazine such as *Emigre* and, due to an ever-increasing print run, it had become uneconomical. After *Emigre* 4 was published, VanderLans decided to change printers. The following issues would all be printed at Lompa Printing, where VanderLans was allowed easy access to the stripping room and printing presses. From that point on, almost all the work produced by Emigre Graphics, including work for outside clients, was now printed at Lompa Printing.

The involvement with prepress significantly changed VanderLans's approach to design. Projects were now designed with the stripping in mind and it became a challenge to make the most out of one or two colors, while spending a minimum on negatives. The results were often monochrome-looking designs, which, combined with the Emigre typefaces, created a recognizable visual characteristic.

Positively Palmtree booklet. **1985.**

Designed by Rudy VanderLans

Poster *"Emigre Magazine"* printed onto untrimmed
Positively Palmtree print sheets. **1985.**

Designed by Rudy VanderLans.

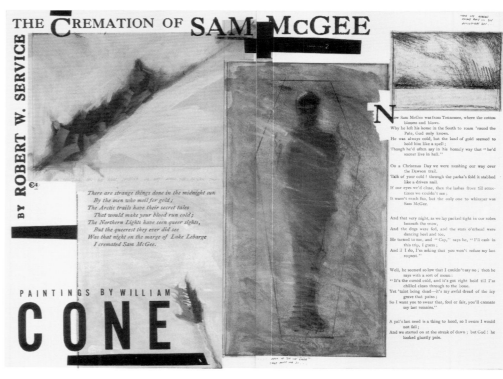

Page spread. Emigre 4. **1986.**

Designed by Rudy VanderLans. Illustrations by William Cone.

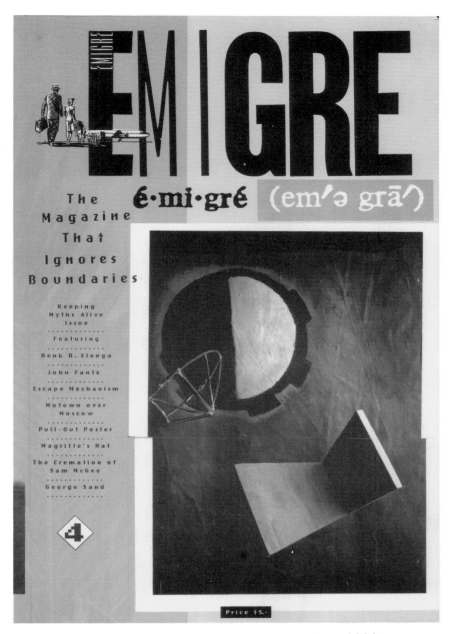

Cover. *Emigre* 4. featuring one of Henk Elenga's staged photographs. **1986.**

Designed by Rudy VanderLans.

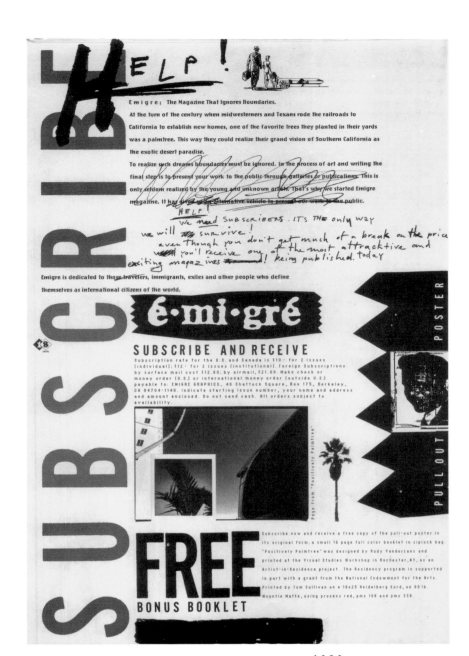

Page from *Emigre* 4 advertising subscriptions. **1986.**

Designed by Rudy VanderLans.

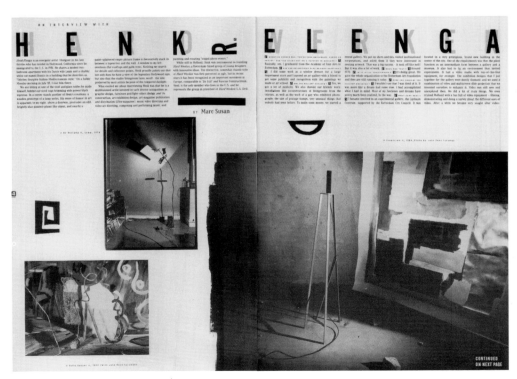

Page spread. *Emigre* 4. **1986.**

Designed by Rudy VanderLans.

Page spread. *Emigre* 4. **1986.**

Designed by Rudy VanderLans. Illustration by John Hersey.

Page spread. *Emigre* 4. **1986.**

Designed by Rudy VanderLans.

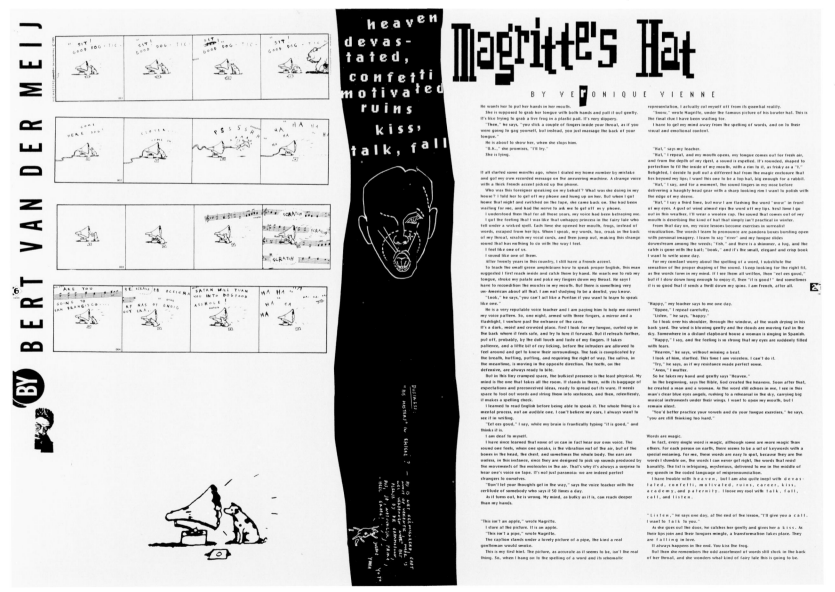

Page spreads, *Emigre* 4. **1986.**

Designed by Rudy VanderLans.

Emigre magazine was being worked on late at night and during weekends. It was losing money and was published primarily as a diversion. Response to the first four issues, especially from graphic designers, although not always positive, was at least emotional. Some immediately dismissed the magazine as being self-indulgent and hard to read, while others were intrigued and praised the skillful use of dot-matrix computer type and welcomed the exposure of a new generation of talented artists. With each issue more copies were sold, encouraging VanderLans to continue publishing. Menno Meyjes had moved to Los Angeles after his first big success as a screenwriter; he had received an Oscar nomination for his screenplay of *The Color Purple*. Soon after, Marc Susan also moved to Los Angeles, leaving *Emigre* in the hands of VanderLans and Licko.

In 1987 VanderLans quit his job for the *San Francisco Chronicle* entirely and, together with Licko, started working under the name Emigre Graphics. Licko continued working for a small group of steady clients including the University of California at Berkeley, but became increasingly disappointed with graphic design and the drudgery of dealing with clients' wishes and the inevitable compromises. Instead she focused her energies on developing her digital-type library, and worked free-lance editing screenfonts for the newly founded Silicon Valley-based type foundry Adobe Systems, Inc.

There was never much collaboration in the office. Each designer worked on his or her own projects, but each made suggestions about the other's efforts. Given Licko's rational approach and VanderLans's growing need to work more intuitively, it seemed best to work separately. The work started to merge as VanderLans increasingly began to use the fonts that Licko designed.

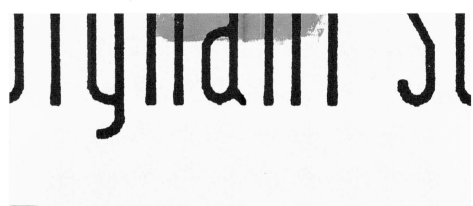

Back and front of a poster for Artspace gallery. **1987.**

Designed by Rudy VanderLans.

Back and front of invitation for an *Emigre* Xmas party. **1986.**

Designed by Rudy VanderLans.

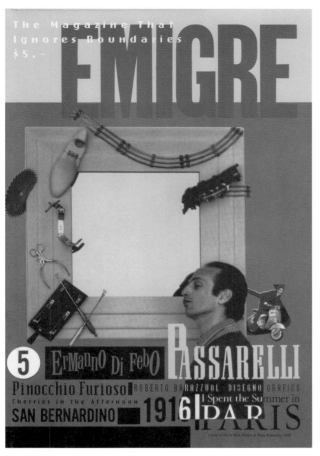

Cover. *Emigre* 5. **1986.**

Designed by Rudy VanderLans. Photograph by Mark Farbin.

Page spread. *Emigre* 5. **1986.**

Designed by Rudy VanderLans. Illustrations by Didier Cremieux.

Page spread. *Emigre* 5. **1986.**

Designed by Rudy VanderLans.

Soon, other designers began to notice Licko's typeface designs, now frequently used in *Emigre* magazine and other designs created by Emigre Graphics for outside clients. Continual requests for these fonts led to Emigre's decision to make the fonts available on disk. After all, with the Macintosh, type manufacturing was a realistic possibility since infinite copies of the typefaces could be made by simply copying the data from a master onto disks. The manufacturing of typefaces was not the exclusive property of type foundries anymore. Licko's primarily low-resolution fonts were initially marketed through *Emigre* magazine. They were used in its layouts and advertised in separate ads that first appeared in *Emigre* 3.

With the introduction of PostScript outlines in 1985, bitmap fonts became technically obsolete, but Licko felt that their designs were still valid. She argued that even though higher-resolution screens and output devices would soon be available, low resolution would always be more affordable and that those aesthetics had to be addressed accordingly. She further argued that coarse-resolution manifestations were the essence of the digital medium, but that these images have yet to be assimilated into our visual vocabulary.

Although PostScript allowed for unlimited freedom in the creation of outline shapes, Licko felt more comfortable using simple circular and diagonal lines. The small 9" screen of the first Macintosh computers forced you into viewing the letter shapes either at a small size, resulting in a crude image, or by zooming into a detail, which made it difficult to render flowing curves. By using geometric shapes, it was possible to conceptualize the letter shape, even with crude drawing tools and a small screen. She based the design of her new, high-resolution, PostScript fonts on the basic principles of the bitmap typefaces, some simply by letting the LaserWriter smooth out the bitmap jaggies, and others by using the bitmaps as skeletons and slightly altering their shapes. Thus she was creating an ever-growing library of highly personal fonts.

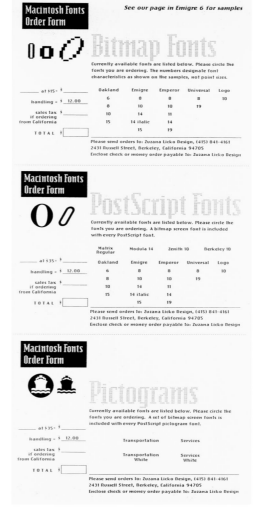

Order form Macintosh Fonts. **1985.**

Designed by Zuzana Licko.

Advertisement for Emigre's digital typesetting services. Published in *Emigre* 4. **1985.**

Designed by Zuzana Licko.

Need

"The design of custom fonts for EMIGRE magazine grew out of our need for unique and more effective fonts than those originally available for the Macintosh. Being primarily graphic designers, rather than calligraphers, we were free of many preconceptions that can hinder more traditional type designers in assimilating this new technology. We enjoy the ability to test and implement the faces directly within our design work.

"With the introduction of PostScript outlines, bitmap fonts became technically obsolete, although their designs were still valid. The first high-resolution Emigre Fonts are based on basic principles of the bitmap designs. Some are a direct outcome of smooth bitmaps."

(Zuzana L)

As a shortcut to increasing the resolution of bitmap typefaces from screen to printer, some programs offer a "smooth" routine that polishes stairstep pixels into smooth diagonal and circular segments. The smooth printing option provided by the Macintosh was the inspiration for the Modula family.

Modula
Citizen
Triplex

PostScript typeface designs. Top to bottom: Modula Light,
Citizen, and Triplex Light. **1985.**

Designed by Zuzana Licko.

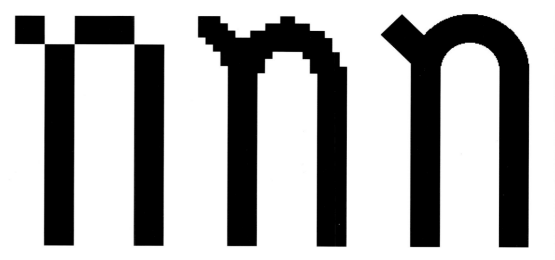

Left to right: Bitmap screen font (Emperor Fifteen, screen font). Smooth printing of bitmap, enlarged 2,375% (Emperor Fifteen, smooth printing). The resulting Modula face (Modula Regular, high resolution).

The smooth printing option provided by the Macintosh processed 72 dpi bitmaps into 300 dpi bitmaps, thereby creating the illusion of high-resolution printing. Deriving resolution-independent outlines for use on photo typesetters left plenty of room for interpretation. Enough room, that three different faces resulted. Modula is a purely geometric derivation, Triplex is a humanist text adaptation, and Citizen was designed to reflect the coarse quirks of the original laser prints.

MODULA REGULAR:
AaBbCcDdEe FfGgHhIiJjK
kLlMmNnOoPpQqRrSsTtUuVvW wXxYyZz 1234567890

MODULA BOLD: AaBb
CcDd EeFfGgHhIiJjKkLlMmNnOoPp
QqRrSsTtUuVvWwXxYyZz1 [234567890]

MODULA BLACK: AaBbCc
DdEeFfGgHhIiJjKkLlMmNnOoPpQqRrSs
TtUuVvWwXxYyZz1234567 890 ? ?

MODULA SERIF: AaBbCcDd
Ee FfGgHhIiJjKkLlMmNnO o [PpQqRrSsTtUuVvWw
XxYyZz] 1234567890

MODULA SERIF BOLD:
AaBbCcDdEeFfGg
HhIiJjKkLlMmNnOoPpQqRrSsTtU
uVvWwXxYyZz 1234567890

MODULA SERIF BLACK:
AaBbCcDdEeFfGgHhIiJjKkLlM
mNnOoPpQqRrSsTtUuVvWwXxYyZz12345678
&90

PostScript typeface designs. Top to bottom: Modula Regular,
Modula Bold, Modula Black, Modula Serif, Modula Serif Bold,
Modula Serif Black. **1986.**
Designed by Zuzana Licko.

Citizen Light: AaBbCcD-dEeFfGgHhIiJjKkLlMmNnOoPpQqRrSsTtUuVvWwXxYyZz1234567890

Citizen Bold:AaBbCcDdEeFfGgHhIiJjKkLlMmNnOoPpQqRrSsTtUuVvWwXxYyZz12(34567890)

PostScript typeface designs. Top to bottom: Citizen Light and Citizen Bold. **1990.**

Designed by Zuzana Licko.

AaBbCcDdEeFfGgHhIiJjKkLlMmNnOoPpQqRrSsTtUuVvWwXxYyZz 1234567890

Advertisement introducing Citizen. Published in *Emigre* 15. **1990.**

Designed by Rudy VanderLans

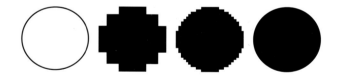

Left to right: Universal Eight, bitmap screen font, "Smooth" printing of bitmap (enlarged). The resulting Citizen typeface design.

The "smooth" Universal face was then enlarged from 300 dpi to fit the 72-dpi grid, created as a large bitmap, and again run through the "smooth" printing routine, resulting in a double-smooth printout. This process was infinitely approaching an ultimate design. In essence, straight lines of varying length and angle were being used to create the illusion of round shapes. Citizen was then created in outline form, with straight line segments.

The scalable outlines in a digital font function like cookie cutters in stamping the character shape out of the printer's resolution.

Stigma

"Low and medium resolutions have a stigma of being crude and incapable of rendering pleasing typefaces. Ironically the original letterpress prints from which many of today's popular high-resolution fonts are drawn are actually closer in quality to medium resolution laser printouts than those of high-resolution typesetters. Due to their relatively crude processes, laser and letterpress prints impart a similar randomness to the letterforms. Had letterpress typefaces been adapted directly to laser technology, without the super-clean high-resolution revivals, we might accept coarse-resolution typefaces more readily today. The aversion to coarse resolution is all the more surprising since the digital image has been common throughout visual history. Inlaid stone mosaics, stained glass windows, embroidery, and weaving designs are just a few of the commonly accepted methods that utilize the digital concept of combining predetermined units as distinct elements to form a coherent image.

"Designers of pre-computer eras have constructed geometric letterforms with complicated manually drawn structures based on the circle and square. Surprisingly, very little has been explored in adapting these ideologies to the seemingly appropriate digital medium. Instead of the current preoccupation with digitizing calligraphic forms, it would seem rather obvious to begin with applying geometric letterform experiments, such as those of Dürer or Bayer, to digital technology.

"With today's technology we are capable of implementing these and other ideas of our predecessors to a fuller extent than they ever could in their time. We may wonder whether access to computer technology would have altered the course of Bauhaus or Functionalist ideologies. Perhaps the rationale behind these accepted digital applications may guide us towards a more comprehensive use of the computer's grid and modulation as an aesthetic force."

(Zuzana L)

TRIPLEX LIGHT:AaBbCcDdEeFfGgHhIiJjKkLlMmN (nOoPpQq) RrSsTtUuVvWwXxYyZz & 1 2 3 4 5 6 7 8 9 0

TRIPLEX BOLD:AaBbCcDdEeFfG gHhIiJjKkLlMmNnOoPp (QqRrSsTt) UuVvWwXxYyZz1 2 3 4 5 6 7 8 9 0

TRIPLEX EXTRA BOLD: Aa B b CcD dEeFfGgHhIiJjKkLlMmNnOoPpQ qRrSsTtUUVvWwXxYyZz 1 2 3 4 5 6 7 8 9 0

n f C g H TRIPLEX SERIF LIGHT:AaBbCcDdEe HhIiJjKkLl MmNnOoPp QqRrSsTtUuVvWwXxYyZz (1 2 3 4 5 6 7 8 9 0)

TRIPLEX SERIF BOLD: AaBbCcD- dEeFfGgHhIiJjKkLlMmNnOoPpQ qRrSsTtUuVvW wXxYyZz (1 2 3 4 5 6 7 8 9 0)

TRIPLEX SERIF EXTRA BOLD: Aa B b CcDdEeFfGgHhIiJjKkLlMmNnO oPpQqRrSsTtUuVvWwXxYyZz (1 2 3 4 5 6 7 8 9 0)

PostScript typeface designs. Top to bottom: Triplex Light, Triplex Bold, Triplex Extra Bold, Triplex Serif Light, Triplex Serif Bold and Triplex Serif Extra Bold. 1990. Designed by Zuzana Licko.

With the publication of *Emigre* 6 in 1986, VanderLans had taken his minimal budget to the limit. The issue consisted of three seperate parts printed on two different paper stocks. In order to save money, those pages that did not require quality reproduction were printed on newsprint. Together with a fan, which was printed by hand on a letterpress by Susan King, whose work VanderLans was introduced to during his stay at the Visual Studies Workshop, all pieces were presented in a custom-made corrugated cardboard box. The box was supposed to function both as the cover (the flaps that closed the box were held together by a large sticker that had printed on it the entire contents of the issue) and as a protective mailer. As a result three distributors refused to distribute this issue because the sealed box didn't give newsstand browsers the option to browse. Such practical considerations kept forcing *Emigre* to standardize. Ironically, *Emigre* 6 won a prestigious award in the 1987 *I.D.* Annual Design Review. The jurors agreed that "*EMIGRE* REPRESENTS 'A HEROIC EFFORT' IN PUSHING THE BOUNDARIES OF DESIGN, AND NOTED THAT PERHAPS MORE THAN ANY OTHER ENTRY, THE MAGAZINE ELICITED THEIR ENTHUSIASM AND ADMIRATION." The entry was further cited as a "GUIDEPOST" to what can be accomplished using computer technology, encouraging VanderLans to continue publishing.

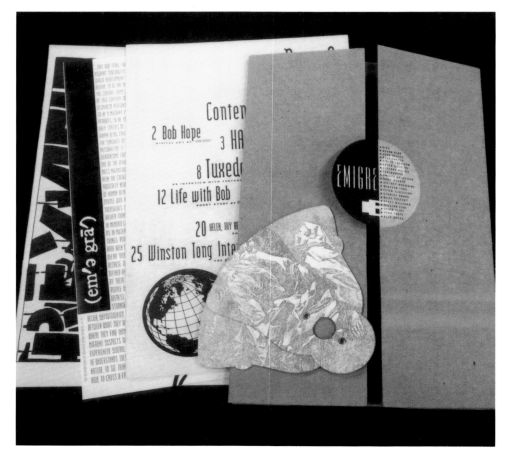

Emigre 6. **1986.**

Designed by Rudy VanderLans

Demands

"*Everybody involved in the manufacturing and distribution of magazines, for economic or practical reasons, has particular demands. These outside forces are to a large extent responsible for the cookie-cutter look of most magazines that we see on the newsstand. Printing presses are set up to print standard-size magazines. Most advertisements are designed to fit standard-size magazine formats. For instance, when you sell 11" x 17" ads, advertisers will tell you that their ads don't come in that size. Advertisers love it when you print on coated paper because they think that it makes their full-color ads look better. Distributors dislike large-size magazines because they're heavy and expensive to ship and take up too much space on the store shelves.*

"*Many of the services that we depend on have particular wishes. Some distributors demand that the logo of the magazine is always placed in the upper-left-hand corner and the price and date right beneath it in 'clearly contrasting colors.' This way they can more easily process the return of unsold copies, which is done by tearing off the top of the cover for proof of credit. Even the postal service has a comprehensive list of layout rules by which you have to comply in order to take advantage of their second-class postal rates. One of these rules is that the magazine's logo must always be the most prominent element on the cover. It is easy to ignore all these restrictions, but it will always end up costing you money.*"

(Rudy V.)

Page spreads. *Emigre* 6. part 2. **1986.**

Designed by Rudy VanderLans. (Bottom) Illustration by Ward Schumaker.

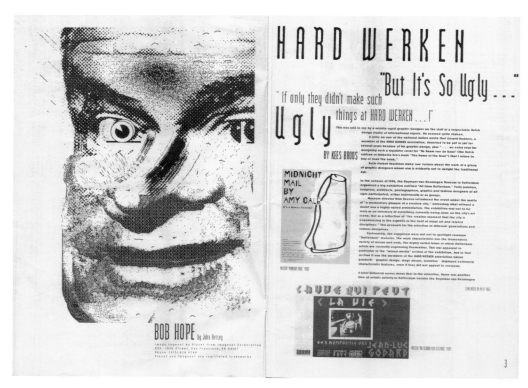

Page spread. *Emigre* 6. **1986.**

Designed by Rudy VanderLans. Illustration by John Hersey.

Part 2

Contents

Contents page. *Emigre* 6. **1986.**

Designed by Rudy VanderLans.

Winston Tong Interviewed
The China of the Mind

"DOUBLETHINK MEANS THE POWER OF HOLDING TWO CONTRADICTORY BELIEFS IN ONE'S MIND SIMULTANEOUSLY, AND ACCEPTING BOTH OF THEM." -1984, GEORGE ORWELL

Interview by Peter Claessens, Amsterdam, 1985. Photograph by Marek Majewski

Winston Tong is an Emigre *par excellence*. He was born in San Francisco of Chinese parents, who met there after fleeing the cultural revolution in China. In the early eighties he took residence in Europe with the band Tuxedomoon and after various trips to Japan he now regards that country as his home: "The culture seemed so satisfying, because it is what I am; a mixture of Eastern and Western cultures counterbalancing against each other in a most terrifying and beautiful way."

Leading the life of an emigrant must add an extra dimension and intensity to one's life. Distant images of the past involuntarily merge with the occurrences of daily life, or in Winston Tong's case, rather voluntarily. In every emigrant two opposing or at least different cultures are prone to clash and thereby intensify each other. Different, even opposing viewpoints, don't necessarily eliminate each other. On the contrary, they give a wider view.

Winston Tong appears to be a very special kind of emigre, not only because he continually exchanges one culture for another as a citizen of the world in the most literal way, but also because he longs for a country he never left: the China of his mind.

I met him after he had just finished his first solo album, "Theoretically Chinese." I caught him only a few days before he was once again off to Japan with Bruce Geduldig, the filmmaker and performance artist with whom he collaborated on various performances such as "Joeboy" and the imaginative show about Billy Holiday called "Franky and Johnny."

PETER: **Where did your inspiration for the "Franky & Johnny" show come from?**
WINSTON: It came from real life. From a situation that I found myself in. I

Page. *Emigre* 6. **1986.**

Designed by Rudy VanderLans. Photo by Marek Majewski.

Licko had discovered a "trick" to smooth out bitmap fonts on the LaserWriter (see page 36). Although it was initially seen as an interesting effect, creating a font that looked as if it was eaten away by technology instead of a rigid computer bitmap font, later it became the starting point for the design of Modula. This precurser of Modula is used throughout *Emigre* 6.

Tuxedomoon's Principle

Often, what is once termed 'Avant Garde' quickly becomes the status quo, becomes 'de rigueur' when Tuxedomoon was formed in the embryonic punk halcyon days of San Francisco (circa 1977), the band was justly considered Avant Garde in its experimental approach to music and live performance. Nearly ten years, numerous records, several labels and a continental move later, Tuxedomoon is still probing its own musical limits.

Tuxedomoon is a band in constant evolution. After recording for the iconoclastic Ralph Records for several years, Tuxedomoon left San Francisco in 1982 for Brussels and a more open-minded and cosmopolitan creative atmosphere. Establishing themselves as one of the most distinctive and successful fringe music/multi-media arts groups in Europe, the band has enjoyed a fruitful career overseas.

As part of an American tour to promote their most recent album 'Ship of Fools,' Tuxedomoon returned to San Francisco for concerts at Club DV8 and the I-Beam in June 1986. These were the first concerts they did in their home town since they left for Europe five years ago. Emigre talked to Peter Principle, one of Tuxedomoon's founding members, about the band's bi-cultural existence.

EMIGRE: Why is it that many people in Holland know about Tuxedomoon than here in San Francisco, your home town?

PETER: It depends on what you are talking about. We are known where we build a high profile. In 1980 we moved to Rotterdam, we made records on Dutch labels, we made a lot of connections with Dutch people, then we were known more in Holland. In '79 we were big overseas here in San Francisco, but haven't played here for 6 years. A lot of people don't know we are still in existence. Also, San Francisco is the kind of place that people move in and out of without staying very long and there is a whole new crowd of people now than when we were last here.

EMIGRE: Why did you leave San Francisco, and why did you decide to go to Rotterdam?

PETER: It's a long story. We were on our second tour in Europe and wanted to get out of San Francisco. We couldn't agree on any place to move to. Some people had told us we could stay in this house in Rotterdam. We got in touch and made a record with Rackthurst Backlash. It was kind of an underground record that we made in their 8 track studio.

EMIGRE: Were you really planning on leaving America for good?

PETER: Yes and no. What we were planning on doing was seeing the world. We never thought we were going to end up playing in Europe for 5 years without coming

back to America. Some of the people of Tuxedomoon have come back on their own, but not the entire band.

EMIGRE: You were in Rotterdam for 5 years?

PETER: No, we ended up in Brussels, because we couldn't find enough work in Rotterdam.

EMIGRE: What did you find in Europe that you couldn't find here in America?

PETER: It wasn't that I was finding anything there that I didn't find here. I just liked it better. I wasn't really leaving for anything. I liked the land there, compared to American food, things like that, very simple stuff. When we left America we were doing fine here and we thought, "Well, let's go where we 're not doing fine." Because it is easy to sail our home small you are, if you think you are big in a small place. So we thought, "Let's go out to the real world." As a certain level, the reception of us in Europe was different from here. In Europe they got more cultural ways of looking at things than America, where everything is based on the dollar. Here it's more like, "How much money did you make? OK, you are a success, it's good what you are doing."

EMIGRE: Do you draw bigger audiences in Europe?

PETER: In certain places yes. It depends on how often we've been there. In Italy we once drew the largest crowd we've ever had - bigger than the biggest crowd we've ever had here. But otherwise it's often the same as here in S.F., or even less sometimes.

EMIGRE: Is the audience appreciation better in Europe?

PETER: We were more accepted for what we were doing in a way, which I don't know is a good thing or not, because now we come back here and we are back where we started from. When we first went there we thought, "Wow this is great, these people here really understand artists," but that's a lot of crap. So we had to play there and realize that the European audiences only wanted us to do what they wanted us to do, just like these people here in San Francisco. And that's good, if I am a paying customer I want to see what I want to see too, it's good, we are trying to do all these things at once, please the crowds and do our own music without being too affected by it.

EMIGRE: What's the reason for these concerts in America?

PETER: We are on tour here in America. We have an American label after 5 years, and we are trying to get back into the American market because there is obviously a lot more money here than in Europe. And we need it. Things are not so easy. "Ship of Fools" is the first record to come out in America in 5 years. This tour is to help promote the album.

EMIGRE: The flip side of "Ship of Fools," your most recent album, would lend itself perfectly to the movies. Is Tuxedomoon involved in doing movie scores?

PETER: We did the film music for a Dutch movie, the name of which escapes me, but the filmmaker's name is Bob Visser, and we are doing another sound track for him later in the season.

EMIGRE: Is that interesting work money-wise?

PETER: I wish there was more work because you don't get paid a lot of money, but it's lucrative enough. Later you can put it out on record because you end up with the tapes for free. You keep the money is not the major factor, that's for sure, but I know Tuxedomoon could do good soundtrack music. Because of that I wish we had an American movie. We have the record company in Los Angeles now, maybe they will get us some movie work. I know we can do that well. I have myself worked on movie soundtracks and Steven Brown has done some movie soundtracks. Everybody has

CONTINUED ON NEXT PAGE

8   9

Page spread. *Emigre* 6. **1986.**

Designed by Rudy VanderLans.

1987 (8)

Between 1987 and 1990, Artspace, a non-profit art gallery and performance space in San Francisco, had become Emigre's main client. Director Anne MacDonald had first invited them to design *Shift*, a new art magazine published by Artspace. It was decided to produce the entire publication on the computer, but MacDonald, who disliked digital computer type, insisted that no low-resolution type could be used. Licko had just finished the design of Matrix, her first "traditional"-looking text face consisting of four weights, with condensed and extended versions being worked on. With its varied editorial contents, *Shift* offered a perfect testing ground for trying out Matrix. As the magazine was being published, Licko worked on refining the design of the font. Many of the following PostScript typefaces Licko designed, such as Modula, Senator, and Oblong, first appeared in Artspace's printed materials.

Shift

In the Stud, on 9th Street in San Francisco, there is a light-emitting diode panel by Bill Bell that plays retinal tricks. It has a single vertical line of red light running up the middle, if you look at it straight on. But when your attention wanders, it catches your peripheral vision, which splays the light out across the surface in patterns created by your own neural wiring. I saw logos and reversed stop signs and things that looked like the monolithic pill-popping light display ads in *Blade Runner*, fragments of the subaqueous narrative that ➤

BY GARY INDIANA

Cover, *Shift* 1. **1987.**

Designed by Rudy VanderLans.

matrix

PostScript typeface design Matrix. **1986.**

Designed by Zuzana Licko.

MORTON'S *Journey*

Title page, *Morton's Journey*, a catalog for an exhibition of Patrick Ireland at Artspace gallery. **1987.**

Designed by Rudy VanderLans.

Berkeley office, 1987.

What you see
What you see
What you see
What you see
What you see

What you see is not always what you get! Computer screens have a coarser resolution than typeset quality printers and the display differs accordingly. Each point size of the screen bitmap typeface is created separately. This is similar to letterpress fonts, where each point size is designed slightly differently to compensate for ink spread and other distortions resulting from the printing process. Low-resolution devices, such as dot-matrix printers, are the ultimate in WYSIWYG ('What You See Is What You Get'), for what you see on the computer screen is exactly what you get on the printout. But readers find it more difficult to decipher low-resolution typefaces on a printed page than they do on a computer screen, probably because the screen display is familiar, being no worse than everyday television.

Perception

"Regardless of resolution, all digital type and images are built out of blocks on a grid structure. These building elements are called pixels and the resulting image is the "bitmap," literally the "map of bits." Very powerful computers are capable of generating high-resolution bitmaps, which are invisible to the naked eye, and are therefore perceived as analog. These high-end devices are usually programmed to mimic existing techniques, such as airbrushing or calligraphy, primarily for the speeding up of traditional production processes. In contrast to this, low resolution is more difficult to mold into familiar form and thus seems alien.

"A common fear voiced by many publishers when faced with using any computer-generated imagery is that it is only appropriate if the content is related to computers. For example, 'It makes no sense to illustrate an article on French cooking with a computer-generated illustration because French cuisine and computers have nothing in common,' but neither do oil paints or lead pencils! Many may also question the use of coarse typefaces, which were designed for the computer screen, in printwork. But again, molten lead has no more to do with reading from a printed page than do laser pixels. It is simply the medium that artists currently have at hand.

"Coarse-resolution manifestations are the essence of the digital medium, but we have yet to assimilate these images into our visual vocabulary. This is truly a unique opportunity for designers to create a new visual language without borrowing from or conforming to traditionally appropriate ideas."

(Zuzana L)

Matrix Book:

A B C D E F G H I J K L M N O P Q R S T U V W X Y Z
1 2 3 4 5 6 7 8 9 0
a b c d e f g h i j k l m n o p q r s t u v w x y z
1 2 3 4 5 6 7 8 9 0

PostScript typeface designs. Top to bottom: Matrix Book,
Matrix Regular and Matrix Bold. **1986.**

Designed by Zuzana Licko.

Matrix Regular:

A B C D E F G H I J K L M N O P Q R S T U V W X Y Z
1 2 3 4 5 6 7 8 9 0
a b c d e f g h i j k l m n o p q r s t u v w x y z
1 2 3 4 5 6 7 8 9 0

Matrix Bold:

A B C D E F G H I J K L M N O P Q R S T U V W X Y Z
1 2 3 4 5 6 7 8 9 0
a b c d e f g h i j k l m n o p q r s t u v w x y z
1 2 3 4 5 6 7 8 9 0

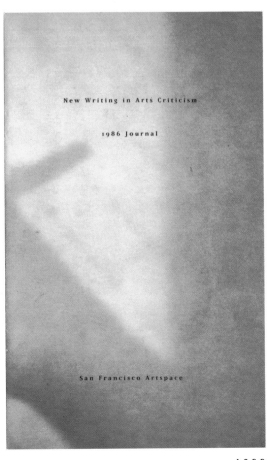

Cover, *New Writing in Arts Criticism*, journal for Artspace. **1988.**

Design and photography by Rudy VanderLans.

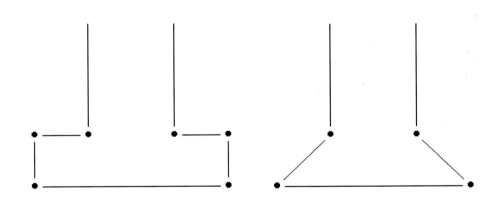

Matrix is designed to economize the use of space for both typesetting and for digital storage purposes. It is one of the most compact designs available; its character count per line is among the highest of all text faces. To ensure legibility for text applications, the basic elements are derived from classical forms. The character proportions are based on a few simple ratios and the points required to define the letterforms are limited to the essentials. For example, serifs with curved elements require more memory than do straight lines. Therefore Matrix serifs are reduced to diagonal lines; requiring fewer points than even square serifs. The 45-degree diagonal, used in Matrix, is the smoothest diagonal that digital printers can generate. Matrix thus consumes relatively little memory space to store in the printer and facilitates fast printing. Memory efficient typefaces were a necessity in 1986, when the state-of-the-art laser printer had less than 1MB of processing memory.

Wide & Narrow

Matrix Wide and Narrow are derived from the Matrix Regular face by proportional scaling: 200% for the wide and 50% for the narrow versions. These alterations add an overall unity: the verticals and horizontals are emphasized and the distinctions among the various letterforms are diminished. The more severe the function, the more dominant is the algorithmic effect as a design element. Matrix responds well to scaling and obliquing manipulations because its forms are harmonious with the digital grid on which these effects are based.

Matrix Wide

ABCDEFGHIJKLMNOPQRSTUVWXYZ12345
67890abcdefghijklmnopqrstuvwxyz
1234567890

PostScript typeface designs. Top to bottom: Matrix Wide, Matrix Narrow and Matrix Extra Bold. **1987.**

Designed by Zuzana Licko.

Matrix Narrow

ABCDEFGHIJKLMNOPQRSTUVWXYZ1234567890
abcdefghijklmnopqrstuvwxyz
1234567890

Matrix Extra Bold

ABCDEFGHIJKLMNOPQRSTUVWXYZ1234567890
abcdefghijklmnopqrstuvwxyz
1234567890

Book Two, Chapter Eight

O N T H E R O A D

Outside Tucson we saw another hitchhiker in the dark road. This was an Okie from Bakersfield, California, who put down his story. "Hot damn, I left Bakersfield with the travel-bureau car and left my gui-tar in the trunk of another one and they never showed up - gui-tar and cowboy duds, you see. I'm a moo-sician. I was headed for Arizona to play with Johnny Mackaw's Sagebrush Boys. Well, hell, here I am in Arizona, broke, and m'gui-tar's been stoled. You boys drive me back to Bakersfield and I'll get the money from my brother. How much do you want?" We wanted just enough gas to make Frisco from Bakersfield, about three dollars. Now we were five in the car. "Evenin, ma'am," he said, tipping his hat to Marylou, and we were off.

In the middle of the night we overtopped the lights of Palm Springs from a mountain road. At dawn, in snowy passes, we labored toward the town of Mojave, which was the entryway to the great Tehachapi Pass. The Okie woke up and told funny stories; sweet little Alfred sat smiling. Okie told us he knew a man who forgave his wife for shooting him and got her out of prison, only to be shot a second time. We were passing the women's prison when he told it. Up ahead we saw Tehachapi Pass starting up. Dean took the wheel and carried us clear to the top of the world. We passed a great shroudy cement factory in the canyon. Then we started down. Dean cut off the gas, threw in the clutch, and negotiated every hairpin turn and passed cars and did everything in the books without the benefit of accelerator. I held on tight. Sometimes the road went up again briefly; he merely passed cars without a sound, on pure momentum. He knew every rhythm and every kick of a first-class pass. When it was time to U-turn left around a low stone wall that overlooked the bottom of the world, he just leaned far over to his left, hands on the wheel, stiff-armed, and carried it that way; and when the turn snaked to the right again, this time with a cliff on our left, he leaned far to the right, making Marylou and me lean with him. In this way we floated and flapped down to the San Joaquin Valley. It lay spread a mile below, virtually the floor of California, green and wondrous from our aerial shelf. We made thirty miles without using gas.

Suddenly we were all excited. Dean wanted to tell me everything he knew about Bakersfield as we reached the city limits. He showed me rooming houses where he stayed, railroad hotels, poolhalls, diners, sidings where he jumped off the engine for grapes, Chinese restaurants where he ate, park benches where he met girls, and certain places where he'd done nothing but sit and wait around. Dean's California - wild, sweaty, important, the land of lonely and exiled and eccentric lovers come to foregather like birds, and the land where everybody somehow looked like broken-down, handsome, decadent movie actors. "Man, I spent hours on that very chair in front of that drugstore!" He remembered all - every pinochle game, every woman, every sad night. And suddenly we were passing the place in the railyards where Terry and I had sat under the moon, drinking wine, on those bum crates, in October 1947, and I tried to tell him. But he was too excited. "This is where Dunkel and I spent a whole morning drinking beer, trying to make a real gone little waitress from Watsonville - no, Tracy, yes, Tracy - and her name was Esmarelda - oh, man, something like that." Marylou was planning what to do the moment she arrived in Frisco. Alfred said his aunt would give him plenty of money up in Tulare. The Okie directed us to his brother in the flats outside town.

We pulled up at noon in front of a little rose-covered shack, and the Okie went in and talked with some women. We waited fifteen minutes. "I'm beginning to think that guy has no more money than I have," said Dean. "We get more hung-up! There's probably nobody in the family that'll give him a cent after that fool escapade."

J A C K K E R O U A C

A B C D E F G H
I J K L M N O P
Q R S T U V W X
Y Z a b c d e f
g h i j k l m n
o p q r s t u v
w x y z 1 2 3 4
5 6 7 8 9 0 % &
? ! fl § ∂ ß ƒ ¶

M A T R I X a new PostScript font from Emigre Graphics.
Available soon from Adobe Systems, Inc.
For ordering and information on typefaces write to
Zuzana Licko Design, 2431 Russell Street, Berkeley, CA 94705.

Text type set in 9 point Matrix Extra Extended.
Headline type set in 96 point Matrix Extra Condensed.
PostScript is a trademark of Adobe Systems, Inc.

Page, *Emigre 7*. **1987.**

Designed by Rudy VanderLans.

Aims

"My aim was to explore two things. First of all, I like to experiment with what the computer can do with things that were not possible with other technologies. I like to design letterforms that work well with the computer, both for pragmatic reasons and stylistic reasons. Because sometimes, not always, but sometimes, you do need something that works well on the screen, like Emperor eight. If you do a lot of editing on the screen or you use the Imagewriter printer, you do, for pragmatic reasons, need a coarse-resolution typeface designed specifically to fit the coarse resolution of the screen. But then, some of my other typefaces look geometric or coarse for stylistic reasons. For instance, Matrix could just as well have had more traditional-looking serifs, but for stylistic reasons, for making it look new, I use a shape that the computer is good at generating. My other aim when designing typefaces is to see how much the basic letter shapes can be changed and still be functional, like the lowercase g in Matrix or some of the Variex characters.

"I am always very intrigued by experimental alphabets that either have no capitals or mix upper and lower characteristics, like Bradbury Thompson's Alphabet 26, or his typeface that has only lowercase and uses boldface characters for caps. This is actually what Matthew Carter at Bitstream suggested I do with Variex (See page 52)*, since there is no upper or lowercase in Variex. I like that, although it is not always applicable.*

"With technologies rapidly changing, traditional type designers are now designing typefaces that they claim are 'device-independent,' meaning that no matter what technology you will use to generate the typeface, the typeface will always come out looking unaffected by the technology. However, computer technology has reached a point where any typeface can be device-independent. This is because of the device, not because of the design of the typeface. The computer, even the Macintosh, which is one of the lowest end, and most popular computers, is at a point where it can faithfully reproduce just about anything. You no longer have to concern yourself with how a typeface is going to reproduce, technologically. You can design whatever forms you like without much limitation from the medium; you can now produce completely characterless typefaces. The question becomes, if we no longer have to be concerned with the technology, then why don't we just re-use existing type designs? We can as easily use past designs just as well as design something else that doesn't have to be concerned with technology.

"I am not saying that only typefaces that come naturally out of a certain technology have validity, although personally I think that those typefaces often do look most powerful, because they were created for a very specific purpose and show real intent. I am bent on making the medium work to the advantage of the design because I find pleasure in that; no other reason. I don't necessarily think that device-independent typefaces, like Stone for instance, are invalid. Although I don't think that a typeface like that accomplishes anything new, I could be wrong. It's just a matter of opinion. It's just that I don't find pleasure in what those type designers are involved in. I'm very much interested in the device. That's where I get my creative energy from. And I guess other people don't. A designer like Gerard Unger, for example, loves curves. To him it doesn't matter whether the curves are drawn by pencil or by the computer as long as they are the curves that he's looking for. He has a vision. I don't have that."

(Zuzana L.)

Special Offer
$5.00

EMIGRE MAGAZINE 7

Various Travel Accounts
A SPECIAL ISSUE FEATURING JOHN ANDERSON, RUDY VANDERLANS, SUSAN KING, ROBERT KOPECKY, TOM BONAURO

AVAILABLE MARCH 30, 1987
Order now and save $1.00 off the newsstand cover price of $6.00.
Emigre Graphics, 48 Shattuck Square Box 175, Berkeley CA 94704.

Flyer announcing *Emigre 7*. **1987.**

Design by Rudy VanderLans.

Page spread. *Emigre 7*. **1987.**

Designed by Rudy VanderLans.

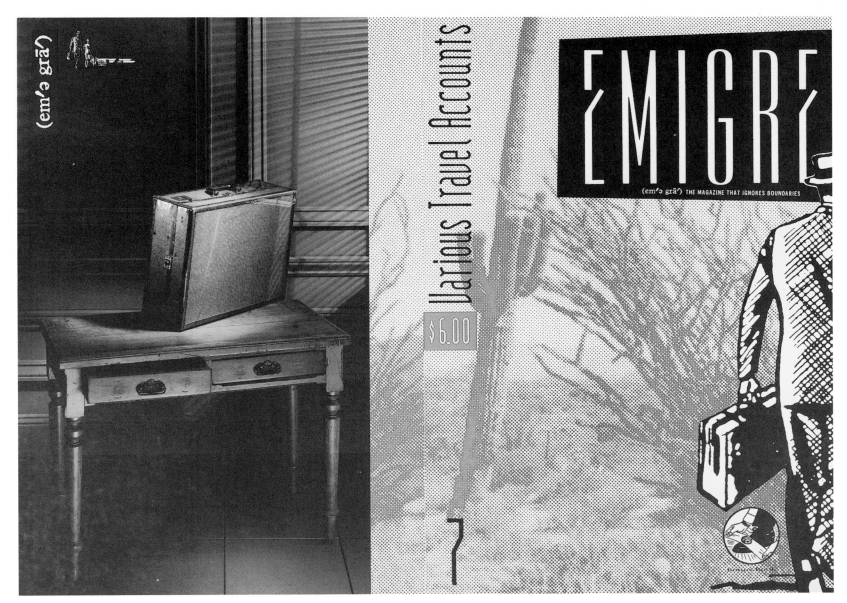

Front and back cover. *Emigre 7*. **1987.**

Designed by Rudy VanderLans. Photograph by Stefano Massei.

Cover and title page. *Emigre* 8. **1987.**

Design by Rudy VanderLans.

Page spread. *Emigre* 8. **1987.**

Designed by Rudy VanderLans. Photography by Stefano Massei.

The "Alienation" issue was a photographic/typographic experiment produced by VanderLans together with Italian photographer Stefano Massei. The issue featured a mixture of type and image experimentations inspired by television and advertising language and imagery. The issue was centered around a single poem by Los Angeles poet Charles Bukowski. These layouts also mark the first time VanderLans used a page-makeup program to create the entire page without additional paste-up, except for the photographs, which were still stripped into "windows" conventionally.

The program allowed for combining numerous typefaces and overlap, stretch and reverse type at the stroke of a key.

Two decades earlier, Wolfgang Weingart at the Basel School of Design had discovered the flexibility of type and image arrangements by using a combination of lead type and transparent film, which offered him "boundless possibilities." The typesetting capabilities of the Macintosh computer, however, made it all practical.

"Sometimes, the computer overpowers the message in our design, but that's simply the price you have to pay when you are assimilating a new technology. We have always tried to integrate the computer into our daily practice. It was obvious to us that we would become involved with computers one way or another, since the entire graphic industry had been moving in that direction. I am afraid that if I don't keep up with current changes, I might end up like a letterpress designer. That is, I could possibly produce beautiful pieces of print work, but they would be extremely expensive. And one thing I've always disliked about graphic design is the enormous amounts of money that you can easily spend without necessarily improving your design. The designs that are printed in seven colors with spot varnishes and dye cutting often don't tell me much more than that they were expensive to print, which is usually the intention.

Explore

"Getting used to the computer was to us, for a while, an end in itself. Especially in the beginning when we had to radically change our standards. Type was difficult to space properly and everything came out looking very coarse. This was nicely balanced by the fact that many new things became available such as the possibility to create unlimited typographic variations at no extra cost. In the beginning, that's what we were involved in; just figuring out how it all worked. What was produced sometimes had more to do with our exploration of trying to figure out the Mac than solving communication problems. Although in the past few years, I feel that the computer has become almost entirely invisible and you often can't tell whether something was produced on the Macintosh or not."

(R u d y V.)

I pour a
drink
into
it

Page spread. *Emigre* 8. **1987.**

Design by Rudy VanderLans. Photography by Stefano Massei.

my head is
still
on

Page spread. *Emigre* 8. **1987.**

Design by Rudy VanderLans. Photography by Stefano Massei.

In 1986 Emigre was invited by GlasHaus, a bi-weekly San Francisco-based party event, to help design and produce a calendar for 1987. GlasHaus was one of the first party events in San Francisco to happen only every other weekend, each time in a different location, consistently attracting two to three thousand visitors. A precurser to what became rave parties, it was hugely successful due to its multi-event setup. The calendar was meant to be given away for free during the 1986 New Year party. Financing for the design and printing was to come from twelve local advertisers; one advertiser for each month of the year. The twelve ads were sold quickly among local fashion stores and hairstylists who acknowledged the GlasHaus audience as a perfect group toward which to direct their advertising.

Impressed by how easy it was to sell ads for the Glas-Haus calendar, Emigre approached the organizers of Glas-Haus with the idea to publish a GlasHaus magazine. Emigre had seriously tried selling ads to finance the production of their magazine, but were unsuccessful, mostly due to the fact that *Emigre* had an undefined audience. Says VanderLans, "EVERYBODY CAN PUT TOGETHER AND PRINT A MAGAZINE. THERE'S NOTHING TO IT. IT'S EASY TO LOSE MONEY. THE TRICK IS TO FIND AN AUDIENCE WHO WOULD WANT IT, AND AN ADVERTISING BASE TO SUSTAIN IT." GlasHaus, with its thousands of patrons, provided an instant audience. A hip, fashion-conscious audience for which advertisers were easy to find. The magazine was intended as an event in itself, a two-dimensional extension of the GlasHaus "experience," which usually featured an eclectic mix of fashion shows, art installations, live music, d.j's, and dancing. Emigre proposed to do the magazine as a three-issue project. If after three issues it wasn't successful financially, the project would be canceled. Together with

GlasHaus letterhead. **1987.**

Designed by Rudy VanderLans.

Business card. **1987.**

Designed by Rudy VanderLans.

Postcard. **1987.**

Designed by Rudy VanderLans. Photography by Joegh Bullock.

Outside front and back of a folder used as a press kit. **1987.**

Designed by Rudy VanderLans. Photography by Joegh Bullock.

event organizers Ermanno DiFebo, Mary Podgursky, Marcia Crosby, and Joegh Bullock, weekly meetings were organized to discuss editorial content and ad sales. Pictorial and editorial contributions came from the publishers themselves and their friends, including photographer Stefano Massei, illustrator John Hersey, designer Tom Bonauro, and many other local talents.

The magazine was produced and designed by VanderLans at the Emigre office. Due to the nature of the contents, which was haphazardly organized and which constantly changed during production, VanderLans used an improvisational, collage-like design style, which changed drastically from page to page and from issue to issue in order to realize the rough ideas of the four publishers. All writing, editing, and typesetting was created on the Macintosh. Texts were printed out in galleys on the LaserWriter at twice the size and then reduced down on the stat camera to generate a sharp, typeset-like quality. The stats were then pasted down conventionally onto paste-up boards.

Ten thousand copies were printed of each issue, and given away during the GlasHaus events and further distributed throughout the greater Bay Area. Since the magazine had no cover price, copies disappeared within hours from being dropped off at the various coffee houses, hair salons, and clothing stores. Due to its instant popularity (partially due to the fact that it was free), ads were sold quite easily and after three issues *GlasHaus* broke even financially. However, the energy it took to keep the operation profitable proved too much for all involved, and after three issues, which were all published in 1987, the publishers decided to discontinue.

Cover, *GlasHaus 1.* **1987.**

Designed by Rudy VanderLans. Photography by Mary Podgursky.

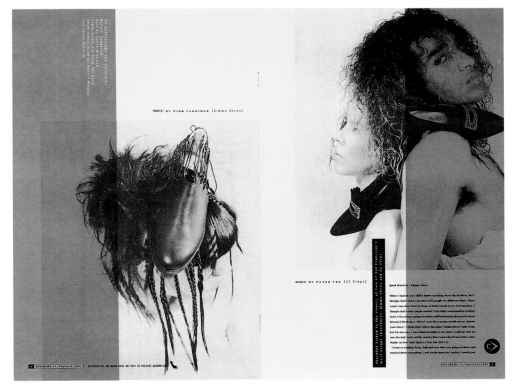

Cover, *GlasHaus 2.* **1987.**

Designed by Rudy VanderLans. Photography by Mary Podgursky.

Two page spreads. (top) *GlasHaus 1.* (bottom) *GlasHaus 2.* **1987.**

Designed by Rudy VanderLans. Photography by Mary Podgursky.

Cover, *GlasHaus* 3. **1987.**

Designed by Rudy VanderLans. Photography by Mary Podgursky.

GlasHaus **3** was designed to function as a calendar. One spread per month, each featuring a work of art created by a local artist and sponsored by a local business.

Page spread, *GlasHaus* 3. **1987.**

Designed by Rudy VanderLans. Photography by Doris Boris Berman.

Indulge

"I've always wondered what this magazine was truly about. Mostly it was about everything that people can easily do without. It was about fashion, what shoes to wear, and how you could present these shoes in the most peculiar way. I always thought it was entirely self-indulgent, without any redeeming qualities whatsoever, yet we were able to print 10,000 copies each time, which were completely devoured by its intended readers. It made me realize how powerful publishing can really be. As long as you cater to their interests, people will read anything."

(Rudy V.)

Boredom breeds innovation. GlasHaus (The Manifesto). 1) Innovation comes by exertion or by chance. **2)** The most blase will exert the most. **3)** In the only hierarchy permissible in entertainment the audience is paramount; next come performers and creators, followed by impresarios . Then there is the rest of the world. **4)** Audience satisfaction is nurtured by an ability to trust and by curiosity. **5)** A multiple and simultaneous performance format engenders a confusion which keeps the audience constantly turning from one input to another. Alternating loci of attention and breaking down the barriers between performer and viewer lead to unpredictable interaction between the seer and the seen, which in turn induces interaction within the audience itself. **6)** Any performance is an ephemeral gift to the audience. A "two dimensional" performance, conversely, can be a permanent gift to an ephemeral audience. **7)** The ordinary presented as performance seen from an alien point of view is more appealing than the highest quality presentation of the traditional. **8)** Liberation of the venue, allowing access to back hallways and upstairs rooms or even outside the parameters of four walls takes away focus from a stage, making the entire venue itself a stage, where spontaneous performance makes the audience itself a star. **9)** Details often leave the most lasting impression. **10)** Punography is a trigger mechanism. **11)** Entertainment is derived from the manipulation of the concept of entertainment. **12)** Style comes from an insurpressable urge to express...as does a certain degree of madness. **13)** In a community struggling to establish a contemporary identity as dynamic and unique as that it has enjoyed previously, continuity and vision must come by intent rather than by default. **14)** The entertainment spectrum has a perfect coverage in a blend of poetry and business. **Brook Fuller**

The GlasHaus Manifesto, *GlasHaus* 3. **1987.**

Designed by Rudy VanderLans. Written by Brook Fuller.

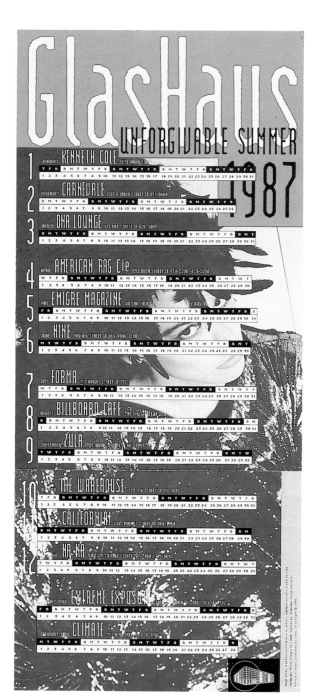

GlasHaus calendar. **1986.**

Designed by Rudy VanderLans. Photography by Mary Podgursky.

Berkeley office, 1987.

1988 (9)

Soon after *GlasHaus* magazine was discontinued, Emigre was invited by Artspace Gallery in San Francisco to design *Shift* magazine. Artspace, a non-profit art gallery and performance space, had become one of San Francisco's major gallery and experimental performance spaces featuring shows by both local and internationally known artists. Artspace also offered grant programs for sculpture, painting, and art criticism. Over the years, through the many personal contacts with the artists and art critics, proficient material of all kinds was compiled, leading up to Artspace director Anne MacDonald's decision to start a magazine.

Intended as an independent outlet for art criticism, reviews, and interviews with artists, *Shift* also featured original art projects created for the magazine by such diverse artists as Tom Marioni, Karen Finley, Gary Panter, Michael Tracy, and others. Their contributions ranged from poster inserts to page sequences designed specifically for offset printing, to cover designs, providing *Shift* with an ever-unpredictable presence and demanding from its art director an easily adjustable design format.

With a minimal budget available and an editorial staff of only two, *Shift* had to be produced on the Macintosh. Writers were asked to submit their manuscripts on floppy disks typed in Macintosh format, which were then edited and proofread by Artspace. The unformatted, proofread manuscripts were messengered to VanderLans, who would create a simple black-and-white dummy of the entire issue. Often, colors were not picked until after a final blue line of the magazine was shown.

In order to establish some kind of recognizability for the magazine VanderLans choose a horizontal format. Since *Shift* was not a newsstand magazine VanderLans was not forced into using the standard vertical format. He further used vertical black bars along the outside end of each page with bold page numbers reversed out in white, providing a simple yet obvious identifier, tying the pages and the various issues of the magazine together.

Shift

The candles in the draughty church flicker, giving shadows and shapes projected onto the stone wall a life of their own. They flutter like angels, spirits, whispers, sighs: enlarged images of the cut-out objects behind the flames. The people who come in to pray, many of whom are either visiting or in the nearby hospital, confuse the art with altar and light votive candles before the secular shrine. The artist is found at times, mystified, in a back pew watching. It is a living tableau of what he strives to create in his work: art in life, life in art.

From *Shadows and Reflections* by Deborah Wise. Continued on page 6.

Covers, *Shift* 2 & 5. **1988.**

Designed by Rudy VanderLans. Photography (bottom) by Sixth Street Studios.

Status

"What I liked about working on SHIFT was that I was forced to collaborate with fine artists. Their approach to design, although sometimes impractical, was more focused on content, whereas I was often too concerned with surface, which paper to use, what typeface, etc. I was also very envious of the artists' status. Whatever they contributed to the magazine, whether it was a cover design, a poster, or anything, it was immediately declared sacred; the 'art' they had created was not to be touched or changed by anyone.
As graphic designers we have a long way to go to receive such blind trust from our clients. Most of my clients still consider design a totally negotiable item, and have no scruples suggesting considerable changes to my designs at any stage during the design process."
(Rudy V.)

Cover, *Shift* 8. **1989.**

Designed by Rudy VanderLans. Photography by Robert Dix.

Cover, *Shift* 3. **1988.**

Designed by Tom Marioni with Rudy VanderLans.

A PORTRAIT OF THE ARTIST AS CHAMELEON

Seven Years of Living Art: Linda Montano at the San Francisco Art Institute, November 11 – December 19. Reviewed by Kathy Brew

Sean Scully, *Conversation*, 1986,
oil on canvas, 96" x 144".
Eli & Edythe L. Broad Collection,
Los Angeles, for the exhibition, Sean Scully,
MATRIX, UAM.

40

41

Continued from page 38

Continued from page 39

Linda Montano in *Seven Years of Living Art: Yellow/Green*.
Photo: Kathy Brew

44

49

Two page spreads, *Shift 2*. **1988.**

Designed by Rudy VanderLans. Illustrations (bottom) Gary Panter and John deFazio.

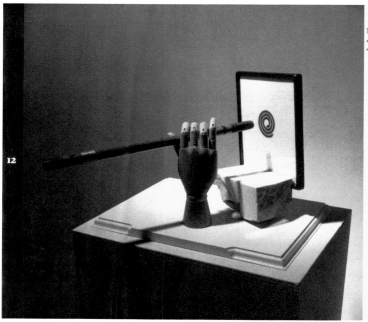

Tom Marioni.
Bird in Hand, 1987, mixed media.
Photo: Paul Hoffman

12

13

PART

2

CONVERSATIONS

John McCarron with *Sean Scully*. Suzy Fartman with *Jan van der Marck*. Kathy Brew with *Karen Finley*.
Bill Berkson with *John Baldessari*. Anne-Marie MacDonald with *Paul Kos*.

Page spread, *Shift 5*. **1988.**

Designed by Rudy VanderLans.

Flexibility

"Instead of setting up a prefixed grid for the placement of text and headlines for all future issues, I exploited the flexibility of the computer. The new page-makeup programs allowed me to design and set up grids within seconds. A prefixed grid helps because you don't have to start from scratch each time you begin to design a page. But prefixed grids can also cause certain problems, especially when it comes to fitting in the texts. SHIFT lacked a full editorial staff, and articles could not be edited to fit. They had to be used as they were submitted. In order to fit evrything in, I soon gave up on the idea of all text columns being the same width and same length. Too often I would be left with one or two lines that didn't fit into the alloted space. Instead I had started to widen certain columns and narrow others to make the texts fit perfectly. In the end I was wrapping columns around each other and creating an entirely organic approach to text fitting. It was a direct result of a new possibility offered by the computer. Although the result was not exactly new. Wolfgang Weingart in his many typographic experiments in the sixties and seventies had created many such layouts, some extremely elaborate. But his were created traditionally and, I imagine, were too time consuming and costly to implement commercially."

(Rudy V.)

Contents page. *Shift* 3. **1988.**

Designed by Rudy VanderLans.

Thingness

Mark Lere: Recent Sculpture at John Berggruen Gallery, May 19 – July 16.
Reviewed by Mark Levy.

Page preads, *Shift* 8. **1989.**

Designed by Rudy VanderLans.

1988 (9)

With all this exposure, criticism was soon to follow, especially in response to the earlier bitmapped typefaces. The low-resolution aesthetic was derived from the screen, but the type was often used in print and people complained that it was difficult to read. Licko rejected that criticism, holding that the perceived legibility of a typeface was strictly related to repeated exposure rather than the method of production.

Regardless of this criticism, the established typefoundries Adobe and Bitstream expressed interest in releasing some of her fonts. Adobe opted for releasing three weights of Matrix but work on the typeface was halted when the Emigre fonts, which were drawn in Fontographer Postscript Type 3 at that time, proved incompatible with Adobe's Type 1 software format. Also, Matthew Carter at Bitstream, who had admired and supported Licko's work from the beginning, offered to release Variex, a conceptual headline typeface designed using strokes instead of outlines.

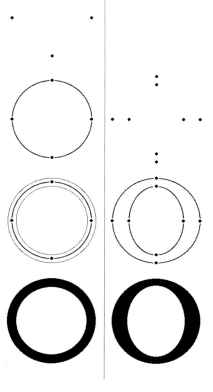

Single-line stroke characters (left) require fewer data points and therefore take up less memory space than double-outline shapes (right). Two separate outlines are usually needed to describe the delicate tapering shapes of traditional letterforms.

Varying the weight of a stroke typeface changes the thickness around the center line and thus alters the alignment of some characters. Variex incorporates these variations of alignment in its design, making adjustments to the center lines unnecessary when changing the weight.

Variex letterforms have been reduced to the basic powerful gestures of primitive writing hands. Elements from capitals and lowercase are combined into a single alphabet. Relying on a single set of characters eliminates the redundancy of uppercase and lowercase symbols. Several alternative characters are provided for headline applications where optimal letter combinations are crucial. Each character is defined by center lines of uniform weight, from which the three weights are also derived.

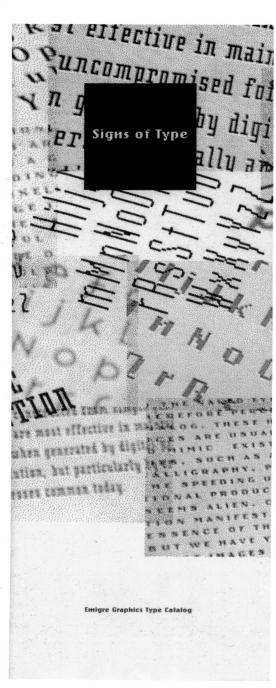

Cover, type catalog. *Signs of Type.* **1989.**

Designed by Zuzana Licko

Criticism

"I have received quite a bit of criticism for what have been called my somewhat illegible typefaces. There are design critics who have said that the EMIGRE layouts are therefore difficult to read. And some have said that all the hyperdigitized type that you see in EMIGRE is an insult to the written language and that it represents language breaking apart. What bothers me most about such criticism is that it implies that within type design and typography, we have reached an optimal plateau of legibility with only room for minor adjustments in detail. This is often backed up with theories and legibility studies that really only tell us what people are most used to seeing. And of course, we know that it is generally accepted that Baskerville is more legible than Souvenir in most instances, but you can never test whether we've reached a level of the best it can ever be. You cannot test those choices that you haven't yet shown to people.

"One reason why people may be uncomfortable with some of my typefaces, especially when used in print, is because they're not used to seeing low resolution type. But why did letter press type start to look a certain way, and why was that eventually accepted? Not because people were reading the type off the bed of the letterpress. They were still reading it off the printed page. That didn't have anything more to do with casting lead than it does with computer chips today, but that's where it comes from, and that's what we've gotten used to. It's the same with black letter, which was at one point more legible to people than humanist typefaces. That's a shocker. I agree with the fact that if you are setting books and other things that just need to be read and understood easily, you need to use something other than Oakland Six. In those cases you need to use something that is not necessarily intrinsically more legible, but something that people are used to seeing. This is what makes certain type styles more legible or comfortable. You read best what you read most. However, those preferences for typefaces such as Times Roman exist by habit, because those typefaces have been around longest. When those typefaces first came out, they were not what people were used to either. But because they got used, they have become extremely legible. Maybe some of my typefaces will eventually reach this point of acceptance, and therefore become more legible; two hundred years from now, who knows?"

(Zuzana L)

variex Light:
AabcdefgHijkLMNopaqrsstuvwxyz
(1234567890)
variex reguLar:
AabcdefgHijkLMNopaqrsstuvwxyz
(1234567890)
variex bold:
AabcdefgHijkLMNopaqrsstuvwxyz
(1234567890)

PostScript typeface designs. Top to bottom: Variex Light,
Variex Regular, Variex Bold. **1989.**

Designed by Zuzana Licko and Rudy VanderLans.

Lunatix Light: AaBbCcD-
dEeFfGgHhJjKkLlMmNnOo
PpQqRrSsTtUuVvWwXxYyZ
z(1234567890)
Lunatix Bold: AaBbCcD-
dEeFfGgHhJjKkLlMmNnOo
PpQqRrSsTtUuVvWwXxYy
Zz(1234567890)

PostScript typeface designs. Lunatix Light and Lunatix Bold. **1989.**

Designed by Zuzana Licko and Rudy VanderLans.

The London-based music label 4AD had provided the Emigre office (and thousands of fans around the world) with some of the most inspiring music to date. VanderLans was particularly impressed with the comprehensive design approach of the label and decided to devote an entire issue to the work and ideals of this indie label which, at the time, was relatively unknown in the U.S.

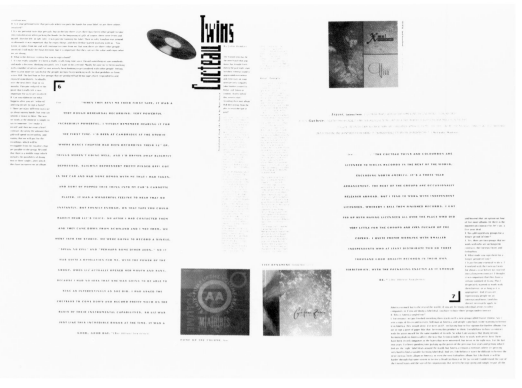

Page spread, *Emigre* 9. **1988.**

Designed by Rudy VanderLans.

Page, *Emigre* 9. **1988.**

Designed by Rudy VanderLans.

Page spread, *Emigre* 9. **1988.**

Designed by Rudy VanderLans.

Conventions

"One purpose of EMIGRE is to experiment with the preconceptions of conventional type design, typography and magazine layout. And you can't change magazine design by finding yet another way to use a pull-quote or to insert an extra dropcap. You're going to change it by writing differently, by setting up the structure of your articles differently. We don't believe you always need a headline, subhead, deck, pull quotes, sidebars, etc.

"We expect and receive quite a bit of criticism for doing it differently, but we also have people who write us letters informing us that, for instance, the 4AD issue was very exciting to read. Some readers almost expected the interviews to be presented the way that they were. They thought the presentation was in perfect harmony with the often experimental work of 4AD. They had no problem with the frequent discontinuity in the text or with having various interviews run side by side. These readers mentioned that they would skip from one interview to the other without any problem. Again, I don't think that all people read in the same way. Today, entire generations are growing up watching MTV and playing video games and it is safe to assume that these people have a high degree of visual sophistication and are not easily discouraged by a less straightforward or ambiguous typography. On the contrary, they are attracted and enticed to read something because of the visual richness.

"We try not to be too concerned with the conventions that exist within type design and typography, because time after time they are proved wrong. We don't entirely ignore all the rules either, because I understand that we are dealing with old traditions of reading habits and we would alienate our readers by totally ignoring all these rules. We would have hated it if our layouts had discouraged people from reading the 4AD issue. Telling people about 4AD meant as much to us as the typographic experiments. If people stopped reading our articles, it would certainly defeat the purpose of the magazine."

(Rudy V.)

By 1989, Emigre's typefaces had started to appear in mainstream design. *Esquire*, *The Boston Globe*, Nike, *The New York Times*, ABC and CBS TV and many others had all bought and were using Emigre fonts. Due to the relative success of font sales, Emigre decided to focus all their energies on type manufacturing and magazine publishing and they ended their relations with outside clients. Their true passion was reserved for the magazine and the typefaces and they felt it was time to explore their real potential, which required full-time attention.

Without the influence of fellow founders Marc Susan and Menno Meyjes, the contents of *Emigre* magazine had slowly started to shift toward design-related issues and in 1989, with the publication of *Emigre 10*, *Emigre* unofficially became a graphic-design journal.

Change

"Ten years ago, we started publishing EMIGRE magazine for ourselves, hoping that there would be others out there who would like it, too. Although this was not an entirely unrealistic idea, it was a bit difficult to find these people. There are no mailing lists available of people that have the same specific interests as we do. Our readers were buying EMIGRE because they liked the way it looked; everyone was always commenting about the design. So after nine or ten issues we decided to change the focus toward graphic design. This was one area that we were personally very interested in and, obviously, so were our readers. Also, the popularity of the Macintosh was creating a new interest in graphic design. Designers from around the world saw this machine as a godsend, probably the greatest thing to happen to graphic design since the invention of phototype. I found myself talking to my friends about topics no design magazine seemed to cover. The entire graphic design and printing industries were being turned inside out and we felt this was an opportune time to start emphasizing graphic design. Also, to increase sales, the magazine had to be directed toward a more specific audience.

"Although we never published an official 'Manifesto,' our intentions are to feature the work of graphic designers that we feel have been overlooked by the major design magazines and design competitions. Usually these are designers whose work does not conform to mainstream ideas or hasn't matured to the point of predictability. They are designers whose work is still developing. By publishing their work, we intend to help exhibit and explain it, and ultimately provide the graphic design world with a more complete picture of the state of graphic design."

(Rudy V.)

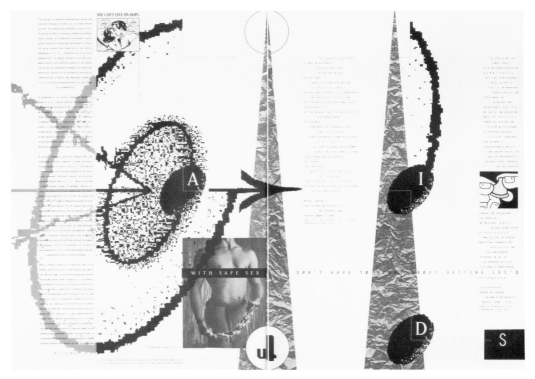

Page spread, *Emigre 10*. **1988.**
Designed by Allen Hori.

Cover, *Emigre 10*. **1988.**
Designed by Glenn A. Suokko.

Emigre 10 was a collaborative graphic-design project produced by the graduate design students at Cranbrook Academy of Art in Michigan and various design studios in Holland, showcasing the exchange of ideas and opinions inspired by Dutch and American cultural phenomena.

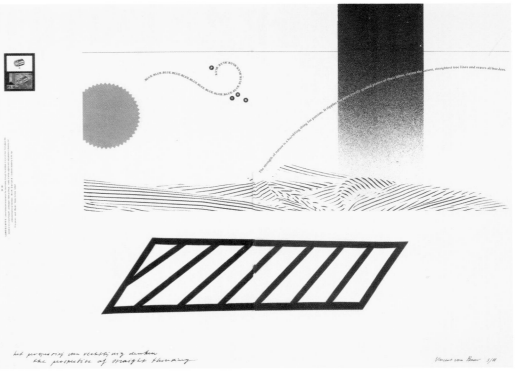

Page spread, *Emigre 10*. **1988.**
Designed by Arch Garland and Vincent van Baar.

Oblong Regular: AaBbCcDd
EeFfGgHhIiJj KkLlMm
mNnOoPpQqRrSsTtUuVvWwXxYyZz

mNnOoPpQqRrSsTtUuVvWwXxYyZz
[1234567890]
[1234567890]

PostScript typeface designs. Oblong Regular and
Oblong Bold. **1989.**

Designed by Zuzana Licko and Rudy VanderLans.

Oblong Bold: AaBbCcDd
Oblong Bold: AaBbCcDd

EeFfGgHhIiJjKkLlMmNnOoPp
EeFfGgHhIiJjKkLlMmNnOoPp
QqRrSsTtUuVvWwXxY
QqRrSsTtUuVvWwXxY
YyZz [1234567890]
YyZz [1234567890]

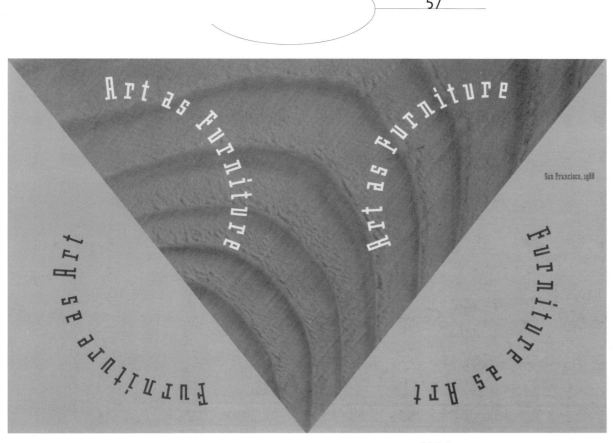

Front and back cover, catalog, *Art as Furniture. Furniture as Art.* **1988.**

Designed by Rudy VanderLans with Zuzana Licko.

Invitation card, *Art as Furniture. Furniture as Art.* **1988.**

Designed by Rudy VanderLans with Zuzana Licko.

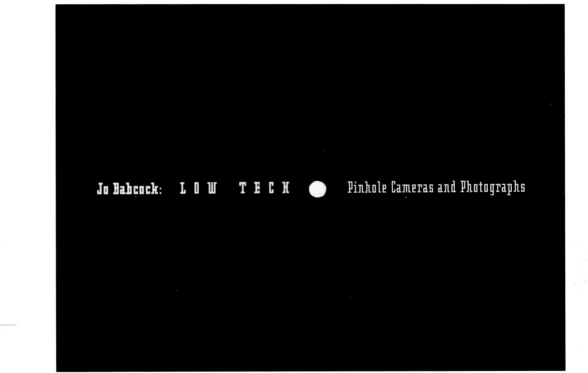

Invitation card for Michael Tracy's show *Santuarios* at Artspace gallery. **1988.**

Designed by Rudy VanderLans with Michael Tracy.

Cover, catalog, *Jo Babcock: Low Tech* for Artspace gallery. **1989.**

Designed by Rudy VanderLans with Jo Babcock.

Envelope, invitation card, *Jo Babcock: Low Tech*, and *The New Narratology* for Artspace gallery. **1989.**

Designed by Rudy VanderLans.

scanned), while at the same time you can beef up some of the more textural things that you might import from other tools. **Emigre:** Are there still things that you find are impossible to do on a computer, but that you would like to do? **April:** I have one problem with the graphic paintbox, and it's not the fault of the equipment. The problem is that I can't afford, either for a client or even for myself, to experiment enough in order to get loose on it. A lot of the work on the paintbox is done with an operator. Now, I have one operator who just sets up the machine for me and lets me play on it, but mostly I have to give instructions like, "Oh, please a little more red," "Eh...could you just move that slightly...." So the graphic paintbox lets me do things that are wonderful and that I need, and the Macintosh does some things

Page spread. Emigre 11. **1989.**

Design by Rudy VanderLans. Illustration (right) by John Weber.

Page spread. Emigre 11. **1989.**

Design and photography by Rudy VanderLans.

Devoted entirely to the Macintosh computer, issue 11 featured interviews with graphic designers from around the world. Inspired by Warren Lehrer's book *French Fries* in which the designer used a different typeface for each character in the book, VanderLans, too, assigned a different typeface to each interview. The various interviews ran alongside each other, creating a notion of everybody speaking at once emphasizing the urgency and excitement felt by the designers.

Various designers were invited to each design a page which read "Keep on Reading." These pages were sprinkled throughout the magazine, functioning as subliminal messages, encouraging the readers to continue.

Writing

"I am proud of the fact that EMIGRE is a magazine published by visually oriented people, especially since most magazines are published by writers, people who are verbally oriented. Among these magazines there are many that have writers or editors functioning as art directors, and I don't see any problem with that either. Actually, this could be beneficial because it integrates the two functions — as long as design does not become an afterthought. It's not that we want to marginalize the importance of editors and professional writers. It's just that we love to write ourselves and we feel that no one can write with more passion about the things that we're interested in than we can. Also, as professional graphic designers we feel uniquely qualified to write about design, since we're looking at it from the inside, so to speak. A large part of our writing deals with documenting what we're doing, almost as an extension of the design process. Our writing might be technically mediocre, but at least we write with an understanding of graphic design.

"I have no aspirations of becoming a professional writer, but the computer can so easily facilitate writing. It certainly has enticed us to become more involved with writing. And getting involved with editing and writing is of great interest to us, because that is what design is all about: information. If a designer can be involved in the creation of the actual information, design and writing can become more integrated. Then, you are involved from the moment of conceptualization, instead of coming in at the end to put on a shine. The Macintosh has given us a great opportunity to specialize in many areas. Theoretically, we can now design type, write, do page layouts, and halftones, strip our own pages, and in a sense it lets us print as well. Whether we have the ability or time to do all these properly is another story, but certainly the computer has made these areas accessible. It allows us to cross over into disciplines that we previously had no way of even approaching. In a sense, we have come full circle. I think that the specialization that exists within the graphic design and publishing industries today has led to a great deal of misunderstanding and waste. There was a time when publishers printed their own books and cut their own typefaces and did the layouts. We are entirely comfortable with the idea of bringing all the separate disciplines together again."

(Rudy V.)

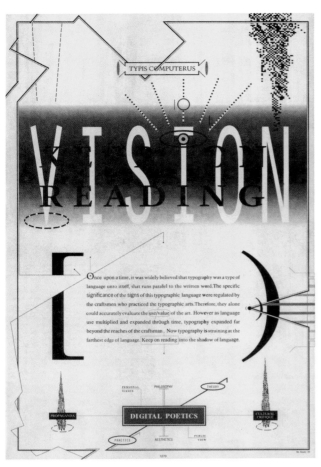

Page. *Emigre* 11. **1989.**

Design by Jeffery Keedy.

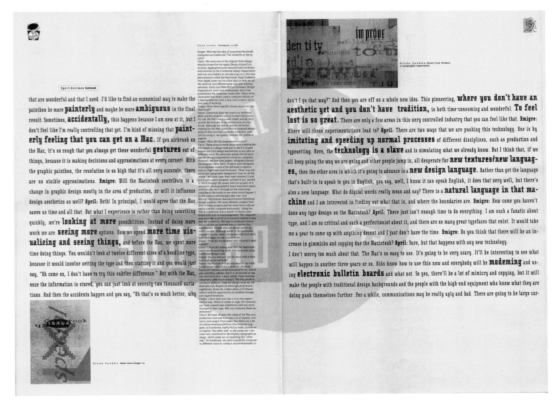

Page spread. *Emigre* 11. **1989.**

Design by Rudy VanderLans.

Page. *Emigre* 11. **1989.**

Design by Glenn Suokko.

Page spread. *Emigre* 11. **1989.**

Design by Rudy VanderLans.

Senator Thin: AaBbCcDd
EeFfGgHhIiJjKkLlMmNnOoPpQqRr
SsTtUuVvWwXxYyZz
[1234567890]

Senator Demi: AaBbCcDd
EeFfGgHhIiJjKkLlMmNnOoPpQq
RrSsTtUuVvWwXxYyZz
[1234567890]

Senator Ultra: AaBbCcDd
EeFfGgHhIiJjKkLlMmNnOoPp
QqRrSsTtUuVvWwXxYyZz
[1234567890]

PostScript typeface designs.
Senator Thin, Senator Demi and Senator Ultra. 1989.
Designed by Zuzana Licko.

Moods

"Ever since I started conducting my own interviews, I have been intrigued with the idea of how to re-create the actual atmosphere or mood of the conversation. Usually, as a graphic designer, you receive a generic looking, typewritten transcript, written by someone else, that you lay out and give shape to. Before I start the layout of an interview, I have spent hours transcribing the tape, listening to the nuances of the conversation, the excitement in someone's voice, etc. Much of the expressive/illustrative type solutions that I use in EMIGRE *are a direct result of trying to somehow visualize the experience of having a conversation with someone. Although this approach is not always successful (some readers are put off by the often 'complex-looking' texts), when it does work, and the reader gets engaged in deciphering and decoding the typographic nuances, the interview inevitably becomes more memorable."*

(Rudy V.)

(WEDNESDAY, JULY 26, 1989, 7:00 PM, LOMPA PRINTING, ALBANY, CALIFORNIA, USA.)

...*RICK:* This is gonna jog to the head anyway, so we're gonna be trimming a half inch off. Did you allow for that? *RUDY:* I did, sort of. All this background stuff will be totally incomprehensible once it's bound like this. The only things that matter on this small booklet are these lines of type. *RICK:* It's printed on a twentyfive thirtyeight sheet. Last time we probably never changed the setups on the lips, so we wound up with a short lip. *ELIZABETH:* So if we're doing twentyfive thirtyeight, and I got a half inch head trim on the film that is provided, does that mean I have to guillotine cut, or do you want me to take that stuff ... *RICK:* No, we want everything with a half inch he **(Rich aaaard, line one!)** trim, even if you have to do a new rule out. *ELIZABETH:* Ok that's fine. *RICK:* Then we should lay everything out and get proper lip from front to back. *ELIZABETH:* Now what about eh **(Richaaaard, line one!)** going to take some trim on the folder? *RICK:* Let's see. It's eleven and a quarter, that's twentytwo and a half, out of twentyfive, that's two and a half inches split between front and back. If you want one and one ... one half ... *ELIZABETH:* Can you run that through the müller? *RICK:* Yes. *ELIZABETH:* I thought it was one and one eighth. *RICK:* We'll have to doublecheck that. How about this letterpress insert? We can run this through the müller without a problem. We'll put the cover on ... or is that too big? We should marry these two inside signatures first and then put it back on. We can combine it **(Richaaaard, line one!)** inside piece. Actually it depends on what that letterpress piece looks like. *RUDY:* It's printed on a ten by thirteen inch sheet. They'll have a three and a half inch flap and it will be die cut in the shape of a house on its side. *RICK:* Do we have a half inch head trim? *RUDY:* No, an eighth. You want a half inch? It hasn't been printed yet. We can still change it. *RICK:* Well, the rest of the book has a half inch. *RUDY:* OK we'll get you a half inch trim. *RICK:* It's either that or we can try and float it in the center. I can float it into the very center of the book...

Inside cover, *Emigre 12.* **1989.**

Designed by Rudy VanderLans.

Advertisement page, *Emigre 12.* **1989.**

Designed by Rudy VanderLans.

The "Press Time!" issue was devoted to the art of pre-press and printing, featuring the work of graphic designers who utilize these disciplines as an integral part of the design process. The issue also includes an homage to H.N. Werkman, the Dutch designer/printer from the 1940s whose work, which was usually created with minimal means, was of great inspiration to VanderLans.

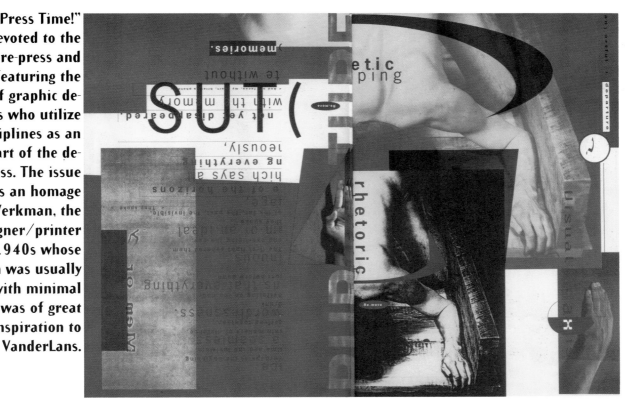

Page spread, *Emigre 12.* **1989.**

Designed by Allen Hori.

It was time for the Big Bens, wooden shoes, Eiffel Towers, lederhosen, cowboys and Indians, towers of Pisa, bowler hats, kangaroos and exotic beaches to move over. For this issue, designers from around the world update their national symbols. Featuring Wolfgang Weingart, Rick Valicenti, Neville Brody, Allen Hori, and many others.

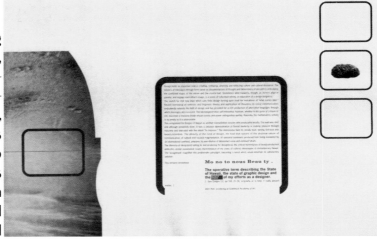

Page. *Emigre* 13. **1989.**

Designed by Allen Hori.

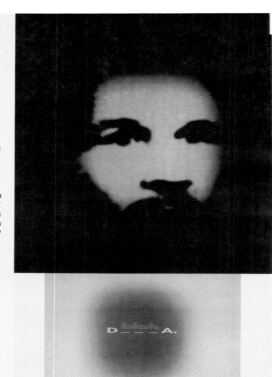

Page spread. *Emigre* 13. **1989.**

Designed by Rudy VanderLans. Left page by Rick Valicenti (Thirst).

#13

Emigre #13. Design and production: **Rudy VanderLans.** Typeface designs: **Zuzana Licko.** Distribution and promotion: **Patrick Li.** Ohio Gallery representative: **John Weber.** Emigre is published not more than four times a year by Emigre Graphics. Copyright © 1989 Emigre Graphics. All rights reserved. No part of this publication may be reproduced without written permission from the artists or Emigre Graphics. Emigre magazine is a trademark of Emigre Graphics. For information about Emigre magazine write to: Emigre Graphics, 48 Shattuck Square, #175, Berkeley, CA 94704-1140, USA. Phone (415) 845 9021. Fax (415) 644 0820. **ISSN 1045-3717.**

SO? BIG DEAL!

Page design. *Emigre* 13. **1989.**

Designed by Rudy VanderLans.

Berkeley office, 1989.

Page spread. *Emigre* 13. **1989.**

Designed by Rudy VanderLans. Illustration by John Weber.

Respect

"Although I still maintain a great deal of respect for the unlimited possibilities of the Macintosh computer and digital design, I do at times feel intimidated by its ever-expanding options. I enjoy using earlier, less complex versions of the page-makeup program ReadySetGo! The particular version I enjoy using does not allow me to rotate type.
"It is very easy to become absorbed by the Macintosh's hardware and software gadgets. I too often find myself tinkering around, trying to figure out new tricks and shortcuts, without a creative thought in my head. It is difficult enough to solve a design problem. Sometimes it's better not having the option of changing your headline into the shape of a fish."

(Rudy V.)

Page spread. *Emigre* 14. **1990.**

Designed by Rudy VanderLans.

Page spread. *Emigre* 14. **1990.**

Designed by Richard Feurer, Peter Bäder, Roland Fischbacher, Polly Bertram and Daniel Volkart.

After Zurich designer Richard Feurer met VanderLans in California, Emigre was invited to a forum in Zurich to discuss graphic design, culture, and tradition as seen through the eyes of a group of young graphic designers, including Polly Bertram and Daniel Volkart. Also interviewed were notables Wolfgang Weingart and Hans-Rudi Lutz.
The issue was designed using Licko's Triplex typeface family, a "friendlier" version of Helvetica and, as an homage to Jan Tschichold, a distinct center axis approach was utilized throughout the editorial part of the issue.

1 9 9 0 (1)

When PostScript was first released and programs like Fontographer made it possible for anyone to design a typeface, many professionals in the design community expected a deluge of "ugly" typeface designs created by novices. However, it wasn't until 1990 that Emigre started noticing and receiving significant numbers of new typeface designs. The submissions came from graphic designers around the world who had observed how Emigre and a few other small type foundries had been able to successfully make available an ever-growing library of idiosyncratic fonts. Ignored by the larger foundries, who considered most of these designs barbaric, non-traditional, and crude creations, Emigre recognized in some of these submissions not a disrespect for tradition but the need for new forms and proportions.

Jeffery Keedy, a graphic designer and teacher based in Los Angeles, whose typeface Keedy Sans was one of the first "licensed" fonts released by Emigre, elucidates on the need for new forms: "AS A DESIGNER I REALIZED THERE IS NO ESCAPING BEING POST-MODERN, SINCE THE TYPEFACES AVAILABLE ARE VERY OLD OR ARE BASED ON VERY OLD MODELS. EVEN WHEN YOU TRY TO DO SOMETHING CONTEMPORARY, YOU RELY ON THESE OLD TYPEFACES AND CONVENTIONS." In an interview published in *Emigre* 15 Keedy goes on to say "THERE WILL NEVER BE A FONT THAT IS AS PERVASIVE AS HELVETICA AGAIN, BECAUSE THERE ARE GOING TO BE JUST TOO MANY TYPEFACES OUT THERE, TOO MANY DESIGNERS WANTING TO DO THINGS THAT ARE SPECIFIC. AND WHAT THAT MEANS IS THAT COMMUNICATION WILL GET A LITTLE CLOSER TO IDEAS. IDEAS ARE VERY SPECIFIC. PLACES ARE SPECIFIC. WHY SHOULD EVERY AIRPORT SIGN SYSTEM ON THE PLANET BE DESIGNED WITH HELVETICA?"

this issue is about type. it is about our interest in the design of new typefaces, and our concern for their legibility and why we need new typefaces in the first place. (all texts in this issue were meant to be both seen and read!) *Emigre*

5

Text set in **EMIGRE**. For more information about this typeface, see the interview with Jeffery Keedy on page 24.

Page, *Emigre* 15. **1990.**

Designed by Rudy VanderLans.

Keedy Sans Regular:

AaBbCcDd EeFfGgHhiiJjKkLlM mNnOoPpQqRrSs TtUuVvWwXxYyZz (123456789 0)

PostScript typeface designs Keedy Sans Regular and Keedy Sans Bold. Second licensed typeface released by the Emigre typefoundry. **1990.**

Designed by Jeffery Keedy.

Keedy Sans Bold:

AaBbCcDd EeFfGgHhiiJjKkLl MmNnOoPpQqRr SsTtUuVvWw XxYyZz (123456789 0)

Mastery

"EMIGRE *15 was a bit of a milestone issue. In it we featured the work of a number of graphic designers who had gotten involved with type design, much like ourselves. As idiosyncratic as these fonts are, we decided to make some of these typefaces available. One reason for doing this is because we believe it's highly unlikely that these faces will be made available by the established type foundries since they are very unusual typefaces not exactly designed according to the Trajan Caps. But we see them as being designed with a great deal of mastery and think that they could be useful to certain graphic designers."*

(Rudy V.)

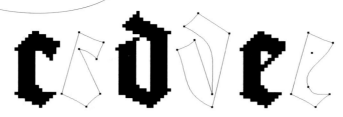

When placing this bitmap blackletter face in the background plane and auto tracing in Fontographer 3.0, several surprising shapes were generated. The essence of these forms is the basis of the Totally Gothic typeface.

AaBbCcDdƐeFfGgHhIiJjKkLlMmNnOoPpQqRrSsTtUu
VvWwXxYyZz(1234567890)
abcdefghijklmnopqrstuvwx
yz(1234567890)

PostScript typeface design Totally Gothic. **1990.**

Designed by Zuzana Licko.

Emigre 15 featured new, original typeface designs and interviews with type designers Zuzana Licko, Jeffery Keedy, Barry Deck, John Downer and Max Kisman. All interviews were conducted by VanderLans. The new typeface designs used to lay out the various pages, such as Barry Deck's Template Gothic (See next page), were still in an unfinished stage.

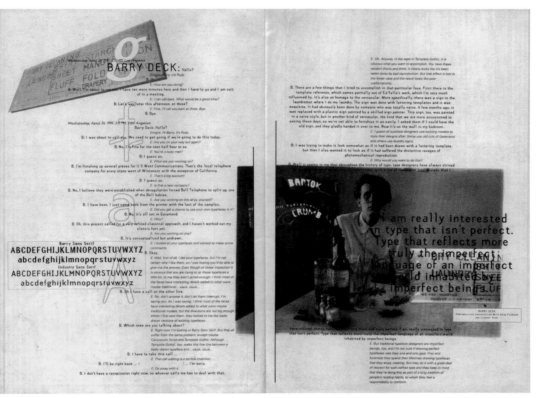

Page spread. *Emigre* 15. **1990.**

Designed by Barry Deck.

Legibility: Letters are legible. If some things are not legible, then they are not letters. Illegible letters do not exist. Illegibility does not exist.

By Peter Mertens

Other methods, including other letter sign systems, exist beside our alphabet for changing sound into signs to render spoken language into symbols capable of being read. It is also possible to create new systems, such as a system of random signs resembling written language in an associative way, which can be used to make stories. It is equally possible to use signs as words or as entire stories. Every structure is language, everything is legible.

Legibility is an undefined notion, yet it is utilized. Researchers have tested the possibilities of creating optimal legibility in texts. They determined how wide a text column should be, how high the ascenders are, what the optimal line spacing is, which typeface presents the most recognizable word shape. They have also found that text in capitals creates indistinguishable word shapes and that serifs create a more easily recognizable letter shape. This information is used in combination with physiological and ergonomic data about the strength of the eye muscles: How often can they go up and down, how long are your arms? The results of all these findings add up to a text set in a serif typeface of 11/13 point with a column width of 57 mm and a 1.5 cm paragraph indent. Sentences cannot be longer than twelve words and there cannot be more than 3 ten letter words in one sentence, etc. This way, it should be possible to create the perfect text in terms of shape, contrast and legibility. The norm can be set. We're done. Of course, nuances are possible and sometimes necessary. Newspapers require a different approach from scientific journals, as do fairytale books. However, the absolute norm can be set.

A system could be designed that would allow the right solution to be found by means of multiple choice questions. Within artificial intelligence such systems exist and are referred to as "expert systems." To make a long story short, the designing of text has been resolved, we don't have to do anything anymore. Every text can be made optimally legible. That is, as long as every publication can be poured into a mould, a universal shape, a uniform. And why not? Why would people — especially those who have taken it upon themselves to transform language into form, to function as intermediaries in communication processes whose goal is to make messages optimally recognizable and legible — not like uniforms? Because typographic designers love to appropriate the Roman alphabet by continually introducing new letter shapes and by making infinite adjustments to the standard. They do this in order to create a specific character and to keep typefaces alive. Since they work within a very restricted area, they sometimes cross the boundaries of what is considered legible. And because of what...? *How der mitte van der mal?*

The typeface that you are now reading was designed by Max+Kisman, a graphic designer/illustrator from Amsterdam. Emigre was introduced to Kisman's work when he and fellow members of the collective WTHe Ambassadors of AEsthEticsSH sent us their magazine TYP/TYPografisch Papier [TYP/ TYPographic Paper]. This irregularly published journal on typography, type design and literature, which claims to be the only one of its kind in Holland, was instrumental in confirming our beliefs that there exist alternative opinions about type and that our own ideas concerning this topic were not entirely alien. The members of the collective take turns in editing and producing each issue, repeatedly succeed in presenting fresh ideas and biting criticisms in an ever-unpredictable and highly original format. Max Kisman, as one of the founding members of this group, first gained notoriety as the art director for WinYL, an independent magazine for alternative music. Punk and New Wave were still in their heyday and the creators of WinYL felt the excitement should be matched in the design of the magazine. Headline typefaces were manually produced, existing faces were modified by optical slanting and scaling, and there was abundant experimenting with photocopying.

Soon after Kisman left WinYL, in 1987, he designed and was art director for Language Technology, a magazine devoted to writing, translating, and getting machines to understand natural language. It was for this publication, which was entirely produced on the Macintosh, that Kisman designed one of his first typefaces, a headline font called L.T.Type. As an early believer in the powers of the computer—before DTP was introduced in Holland, he had already designed a postage stamp for the Dutch postal service on an Amiga—he involved himself with the Macintosh from its introduction. Much of his early work, including the many typefaces he designed during this time, displays the high level of experimentation that he does in order to understand and come to terms with the computer. Which custom-designed typefaces, he says, "You can give a specific identity to a product. That is why and how I design."

Page spread. *Emigre* 15. **1990.**

Designed by Rudy VanderLans.

Poster for the band Every Good Boy using Template Gothic. **1992**.

Designed by Rudy VanderLans. Illustration by Elizabeth Charman.

Page. *Emigre* 18, advertising Template Gothic. **1991**.

Designed by **Barry Deck**.

Template Gothic:
AaBbCcDd
EeFfGgHhIiJjKkLlM
mNnOoPpQqRrSsTt
UuVvWwXxYyZz
(1234567890)

Template Gothic
Bold:
AaBbCcDd
EeFfGgHhIiJjKkLlM
mNnOoPpQqRrSsTt
UuVvWwXxYyZz
(123456789)

PostScript typeface designs Template Gothic and
Template Gothic Bold. **1990**.

Designed by Barry Deck.

AABBCCDEEFFGGHIIJJ
KLMMNOPQRSSTTUUVW
WXYYZ(1234567890)

PostScript typeface design Totally Glyphic. **1990**.

Designed by Zuzana Licko.

Triplex Italic Light:

A a B b C c D d E e F f G g H h I i J j K k
L l M m N n O o P p Q q R r S s T t U u
V v W w X x Y y Z z
(1 2 3 4 5 6 7 8 9 0)

Triplex Italic Bold:

A a B b C c D d E e F f G g H h I i J j K
k L l M m N n O o P p Q q R r S s
T t U u V v W w X x Y y Z z
(1 2 3 4 5 6 7 8 9)

Triplex Italic Extra Bold:

A a B b C c D d E e F f G g H h I i J
j K k L l M m N n O o P p Q q R r S s
T t U u V v W w X x Y y Z z
(1 2 3 4 5 6 7 8 9)

This italic was originally conceived as a companion for a typeface called Arcatext, designed by John Downer. At one stage, a certain customer was interested in Arcatext but wanted a different italic drawn for it. Emigre then saw the original drawings and subsequently decided to commission the abandoned italic as a digital typeface in three weights to accompany Zuzana Licko's new Triplex typeface family.

PostScript typeface designs Triplex Italic Light, Triplex Italic
Bold and Triplex Italic Extra Bold. 1991.

Designed by John Downer.

EMIGRE: Just like many innovative musicians, you attended design school. Where did you go to school?   JAMES: I attended the Columbus College of Art and Design and graduated about five years ago.   EMIGRE: And you're working as a graphic designer right now?   JAMES: Yes, I was just recently hired by a studio here in Columbus called Oxmox Design. Before that I worked in a Catholic hospital. I was their graphics department and designed things like hysterectomy brochures and "Save Your Urine" stickers for old people.   EMIGRE: How long has your label BLACK music been around?   JAMES: About five years.   EMIGRE: How do you afford that? I look at the cassette packaging and some is printed in full color! It must be costly.   JAMES: Not really. I use inexpensive printers and twist their arms f o r t h e s a k e o f a r t.   EMIGRE: Do you sell your tapes only by mail order?   JAMES: Yes. Although I do sell some cassettes through local stores, I sell most copies through mail order.   EMIGRE: How many do you produce each time?   JAMES: Anywhere from three to five hundred.   EMIGRE: I guess you can make them as you go along?   JAMES: Yes. Every time I have a new release, I duplicate and assemble a couple of hundred and after they're gone, I just copy them on a supply-and-demand basis. I send out a promotional postcard to everyone on my mailing list and most people pretty much buy whatever I put out.   EMIGRE: Has it paid for itself?   JAMES: I almost break even with each release. It all depends on how costly the production comes out to be.

EMIGRE: Has any of your music been released by other record companies?   JAMES: No. I've had a few songs on some compilation albums, but that's about it.   EMIGRE: Have you ever actively pursued deals with record companies?   JAMES: Whenever I finish a cassette, I send one to each one of my favorite record companies like Nettwerk, WaxTrax, Mute, and a lot of the small independent labels.   EMIGRE: Has anything ever materialized?   JAMES: Not really. The person from Nettwerk has written me back a few times, and I've written him back a few times, but nothing's really come of it. Usually they ask me to send more material, more music.   EMIGRE: But you would be interested in those companies releasing your work?   JAMES: S u r e !   EMIGRE: I'm asking because it seems like you've turned your mail order business into such a unique thing by doing it all yourself. I can easily imagine that you'd like to keep it that way and remain in complete control.   JAMES: I do get a lot of gratification out of doing it all myself and having the name and address of every single person who buys my cassettes. But I'd love to reach a wider audience. It's a lot of work mailing the catalogs and postcards and filling people's orders, while simultaneously trying to produce music and work a steady job.

In the following paragraph, James briefly attempts to describe the sounds on the Cathode Raymonde cassette. "Pre-recorded audio-clippings synchronized with fat and skinny rhythms alike. Electrically-generated tones allotted their own little spaces in time, of course 'in time.' Anonymous voices pop in and about, like anonymous voices sometimes do. Panning left, panning right. Panning up 'n down. Soundtracks. Foundtracks. Feet-off-the-groundtracks. Technological populogical synth-plop from a to z. The duration of a typical sitcom or a 30-mile drive @ 60mph. Repetitive phrases soak into your sponge-like subconscious at an alarming rate. Toe-tappin' fun the new-fashioned way. Electronic music like good ole Mom used to make. Now if that doesn't sound intriguing, I don't know what does."

EMIGRE: What I like about your music is that it never quite fulfills the expectations it creates. A nice rhythm will start, a catchy melody will develop, but just as I become aware of it, something happens and the rhythm will change or some unfamiliar sound will surface. It's entirely unpredictable. Your music is also very fragmented and layered, very much like a lot of graphic design I see today.   JAMES: The parallels you can draw between electronic music and electronically-generated graphics are very strong. I really started noticing these parallels ever since designers started scanning images. Sometimes I think of my music as bitmapped music - low resolution, jagged

(INTERVIEW CONTINUES ON NEXT PAGE)

For information on other Fact TwentyTwo recordings write to BLACKmusic at 1230 Bryden Road, Columbus, Ohio 43205-1901, USA.

Cover. *Emigre* 16. **1990.**

Designed and printed by Bruce Licher at Independent Project Press.

Page spread. *Emigre* 16. **1990.**

Designed by Rudy VanderLans.

One of the perks of publishing *Emigre* is that you receive a countless number of unsolicited printed and recorded material of all kinds. Issue 16 is a showcase of a selection of the kind of rarities that Emigre found to be inspiring, funny, or significant.

Page spread. *Emigre* 16. **1990.**

Designed by Rudy VanderLans.

Elegance

"Although after five years of working on simple bitmap type designs I have acquired more confidence doing 'humanist' designs such as Triplex and Journal, I've never considered designing type entirely by hand, more calligraphic type. For one, I've never been very attracted to doing calligraphy. With calligraphy there was such a set way of doing things that unless you could technically outdo the next guy it became just a matter of production. How many hours could you spend doing this? That to me was more therapeutic than creative. Also, I'm very concerned with maximizing our resources and not fighting with the medium. We do it in our design work as well. For example, we like to overprint offset colors, instead of knocking them out, in order not to kill ourselves in the stripping process. And that's not just a matter of money, it's also that things look better that way and are easier to produce. Why do it the difficult way, or why do it backward? Simply because that's the way you happen to think and you haven't taught yourself to see things in a more direct way? When designers do things that don't come out of the medium, such as reproducing Goudy Old Style or Optima with postscript, or reversing six-point red type out of a composite 20% blue and 60% yellow screen, when people do that, it's usually not because it's absolutely the best way to communicate the message. I think it is because of their disinterest in understanding the possibilities of the tools, or how these tools can possibly be used better. It's just that they don't think. They can only work within this narrow range of what they're used to. It's all preconceived.

"Look at traditional typeface designers. They think that typefaces need to look a certain way because they are calligraphers, and that's the way type has always been for them. They're content to continue designing the same type styles regardless of the medium they're using. And that's plain stupid. Why do something that goes against the grain of the medium that you're using? That's why I still like to design low-resolution typefaces. It has something to do with elegance. When something emerges naturally, it sits right. You don't feel like you're beating against the current. And that's a feeling that I enjoy. The typefaces I like best in this respect are low-resolution typefaces like Emperor Eight or Oakland Six, they really work well at every level on the computer. You can use them in high-resolution programs and you can use them in MacPaint and they feel just as comfortable."

(Zuzana L)

Low and medium resolutions have a stigma of being crude and incapable of rendering pleasing typefaces. Ironically the original letterpress prints from which many of today's popular high-resolution fonts are adapted are actually closer in quality to medium-resolution laser printouts than those of high-resolution typesetters. Due to their relatively crude processes, laser and letterpress prints impart a similar randomness to the letterforms. Had letterpress typefaces been adapted directly to laser technology, without the superclean high-resolution revivals, we might accept coarse-resolution typefaces more readily today. Journal is an uncommon revival. Rather than resurrecting a particular typeface from letterpress specimens, Journal is a revival of the letterpress look itself. The irregularities that appear in letterpress printing are simulated; for example all curves are defined with straight lines. This yields a subtle crudeness that is apparent in laser printer printouts as well as high-resolution typesetting. Journal also evokes the informal qualities of familiar typewriter designs, making it suitable for correspondence.

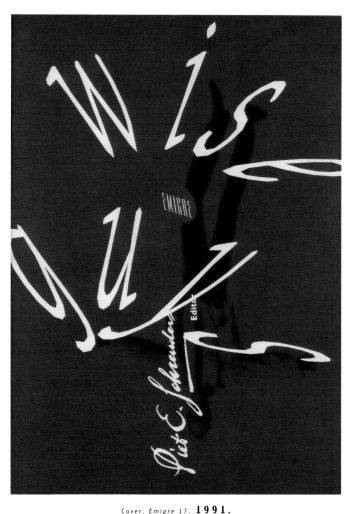

Cover, *Emigre* 17. **1991.**

Designed by Rudy VanderLans.

Journal Text:

AaBbCcDdEeFfGggHhIiJjKkLlMmNnOoPpQqRrSsTtUu VvWwXxYyZz(1234567890)

Journal Ultra:

AaBbCcDdEeFfGggHhIiJjKkLlMmNnOoPpQqRr SsTtUuVvWwXxYyZz(1234567890)

Journal Italic:

AaBbCcDdEeFfGgHhIiJjKkLlMmNnOoPpQqRrSsTtUuVvW wXxYyZz(1234567890)

PostScript typeface designs Journal Text, Journal Ultra, and Journal Italic. **1991.**

Designed by Zuzana Licko.

"There is no rhyme or reason in our selection process as to whom we decide to feature in EMIGRE. We stay in touch with a lot of graphic designers around the world. Whenever we come across work that we are attracted to, we try to become acquainted with the people who created it. Then we stay in touch and wait for the appropriate moment to invite them to contribute in one way or another.

"Once we invite a certain person or a group of people to contribute, they will have free rein. Except for the natural restrictions of the magazine such as format, paper, the single available color, and the theme, they can do what they want and we will publish what they submit, without any interference, editing, or by-committee voting. With this approach we have been able to publish the work without compromising it and in the process we have been able to remain fairly unpredictable, both editorially and visually. Although as a result, I must admit, we have occasionally been forced to publish projects that we personally find absolutely hideous.

"On the whole we have turned down only three pieces, but never on aesthetic grounds. We turned down one cover design, which would have cost a fortune to print, and two pieces, both small ads, were turned down for ethical reasons."

(Rudy V.)

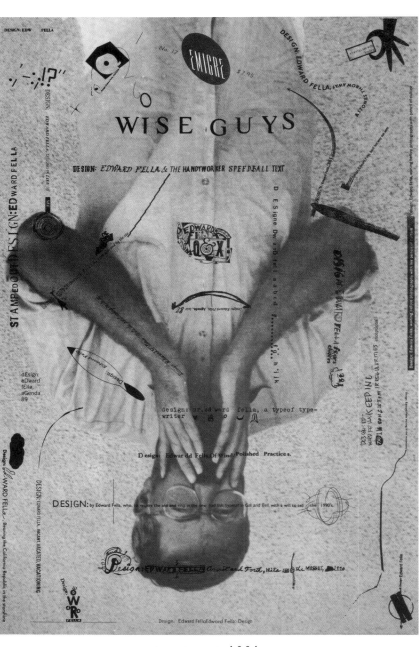

Cover, *Emigre* 17. **1991.**

Designed by Jeffery Keedy.

Page, *Emigre* 17. **1991.**

Designed by Rudy VanderLans.

Page spread, *Emigre* 17. **1991.**

Designed by Jeffery Keedy.

Emigre 17, the "Wise Guys" issue, featured interviews with Dutch journalist/designer Piet Schreuders and American designer Ed Fella. Both are know for their "vernacular" work, and are extremely influential in their respective countries. The issue was split in half, each with a front cover, one part edited and designed by Jeffery Keedy, the other by VanderLans (See previous page).

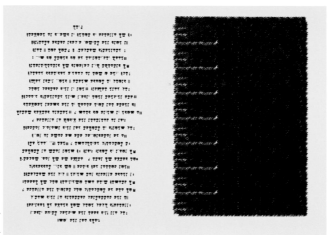

Page spread. *Emigre* 18. **1991.**

Designed by Pierre Di Sciullo.

Emigre 18 further explores the unknown possibilities of type as an expressive/communicative medium. This issue features the work of typographers Pierre di Sciullo, Phil Baines, Erik van Blokland, and Just van Rossum.

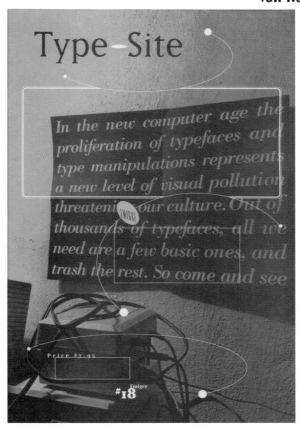

Cover. *Emigre* 18. **1991.**

Design and photography by Rudy VanderLans.

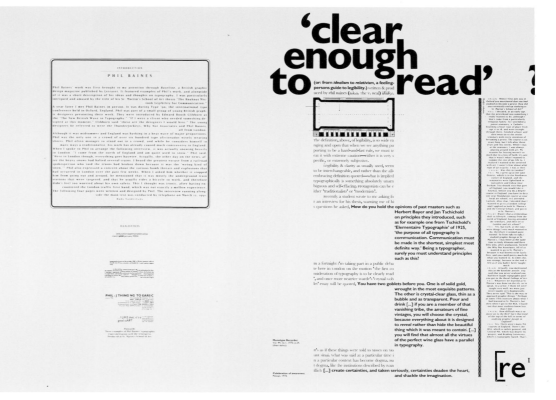

Page spread. *Emigre* 18. **1991.**

Designed by Rudy VanderLans. Right page designed with Phil Baines.

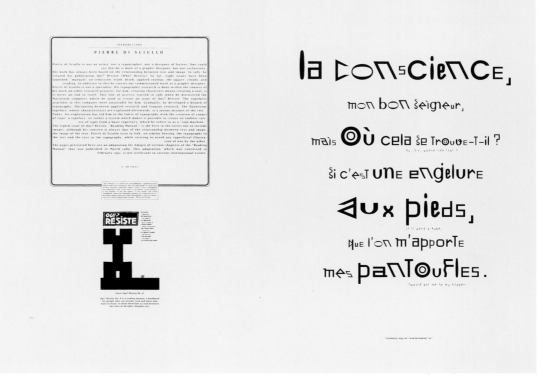

Page spread. *Emigre* 18. **1991.**

Designed by Rudy VanderLans. Right page designed with Pierre Di Sciullo.

Elizabeth Dunn, Emigre's former sales and distribution manager, one day came across Fontographer, a type design software, and discovered how simple it was to "create" a typeface. During two lunch breaks she then created Marvelous, a typeface designed with as much intent and concern for detail, only of a different kind, as any traditional typeface. In the process she has created what some people in the graphic design community have expected to happen on a large scale: typeface designs of a highly personal kind, not unlike handwriting. Although there is much concern over the degradation of type design standards due to the involvement of the uninitiated, Emigre does not think that such designs are contributing to a new level of visual pollution, at least not until such typefaces are used indiscriminately.

Zuzana Licko (left) and Elizabeth Dunn (right),
Berkeley office, 1991.

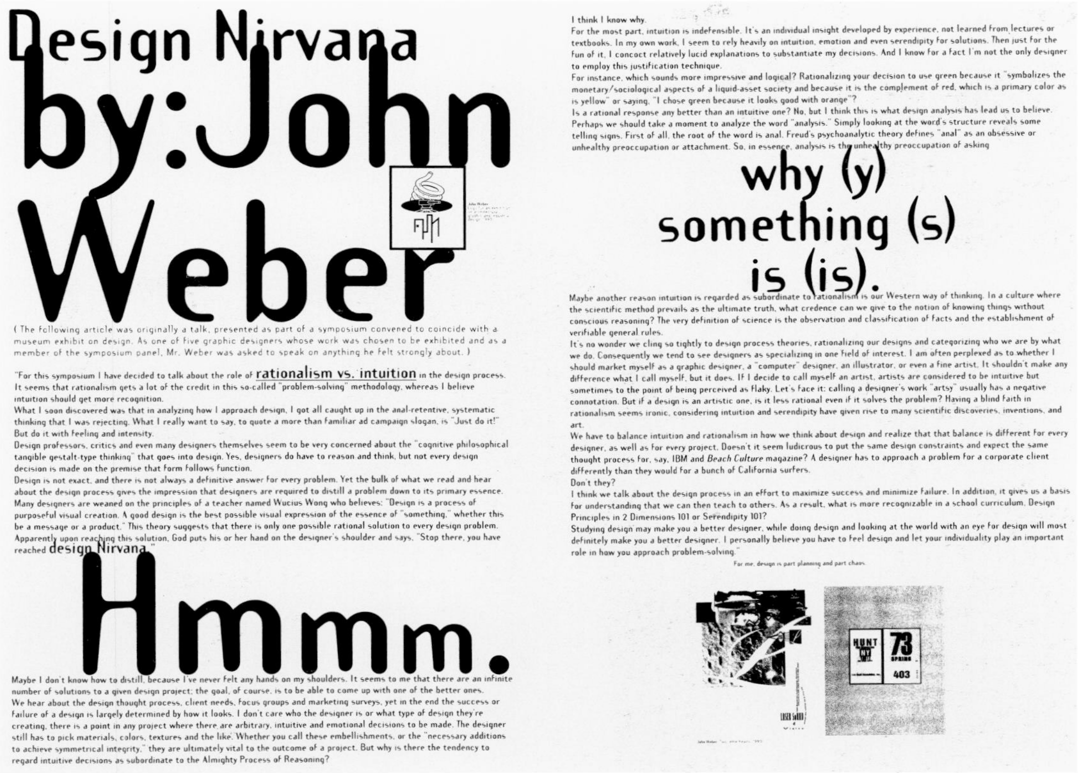

Design Nirvana
by:John Weber

(The following article was originally a talk, presented as part of a symposium convened to coincide with a museum exhibit on design. As one of five graphic designers whose work was chosen to be exhibited and as a member of the symposium panel, Mr. Weber was asked to speak on anything he felt strongly about.)

"For this symposium I have decided to talk about the role of **rationalism vs. intuition** in the design process. It seems that rationalism gets a lot of the credit in this so-called "problem-solving" methodology, whereas I believe intuition should get more recognition.

What I soon discovered was that in analyzing how I approach design, I got all caught up in the anal-retentive, systematic thinking that I was rejecting. What I really want to say, to quote a more than familiar ad campaign slogan, is "Just do it!" But do it with feeling and intensity.

Design professors, critics and even many designers themselves seem to be very concerned about the "cognitive philosophical tangible gestalt-type thinking" that goes into design. Yes, designers do have to reason and think, but not every design decision is made on the premise that form follows function.

Design is not exact, and there is not always a definitive answer for every problem. Yet the bulk of what we read and hear about the design process gives the impression that designers are required to distill a problem down to its primary essence. Many designers are weaned on the principles of a teacher named Wucius Wong who believes: "Design is a process of purposeful visual creation. A good design is the best possible visual expression of the essence of 'something,' whether this be a message or a product." This theory suggests that there is only one possible rational solution to every design problem. Apparently upon reaching this solution, God puts his or her hand on the designer's shoulder and says, "Stop there, you have reached design Nirvana.

Hmmm.

Maybe I don't know how to distill, because I've never felt any hands on my shoulders. It seems to me that there are an infinite number of solutions to a given design project; the goal, of course, is to be able to come up with one of the better ones. We hear about the design thought process, client needs, focus groups and marketing surveys, yet in the end the success or failure of a design is largely determined by how it looks. I don't care who the designer is or what type of design they're creating, there is a point in any project where there are arbitrary, intuitive and emotional decisions to be made. The designer still has to pick materials, colors, textures and the like. Whether you call these embellishments, or the "necessary additions to achieve symmetrical integrity," they are ultimately vital to the outcome of a project. But why is there the tendency to regard intuitive decisions as subordinate to the Almighty Process of Reasoning?

I think I know why.

For the most part, intuition is indefinable. It's an individual insight developed by experience, not learned from lectures or textbooks. In my own work, I seem to rely heavily on intuition, emotion and even serendipity for solutions. Then just for the fun of it, I concoct relatively lucid explanations to substantiate my decisions. And I know for a fact I'm not the only designer to employ this justification technique.

For instance, which sounds more impressive and logical? Rationalizing your decision to use green because it "symbolizes the monetary/sociological aspects of a liquid-asset society and because it is the complement of red, which is a primary color as yellow" or saying, "I chose green because it looks good with orange"?

Is a rational response any better than an intuitive one? No, but I think this is what design analysis has lead us to believe. Perhaps we should take a moment to analyze the word "analysis." Simply looking at the word's structure reveals some telling signs. First of all, the root of the word is anal. Freud's psychoanalytic theory defines "anal" as an obsessive or unhealthy preoccupation or attachment. So, in essence, analysis is the unhealthy preoccupation of asking

why (y) something (s) is (is).

Maybe another reason intuition is regarded as subordinate to rationalism is our Western way of thinking. In a culture where the scientific method prevails as the ultimate truth, what credence can we give to the notion of knowing things without conscious reasoning? The very definition of science is the observation and classification of facts and the establishment of verifiable general rules.

It's so maybe the flavor, the design process, are a different story altogether. After having read the book *Cranbrook Design: The New Discourse*, and seeing the ultra-slick, beautifully detailed, perfectly executed two and three dimensional designs, I was inspired to see the environment in which these were created. I can't explain exactly what I had expected, but the last thing I had in mind was the image of a hippy commune in northern Oregon during the early 1970's. But that's about as well as I can describe it. There were dogs running around, people sitting on a square inch of unused table space. The place was packed with couches, mattresses, chairs, books, pots and pans, dog bowls, computers, all haphazardly partitioned with makeshift panels and drapecloth curtains I was impressed.

Page spread, *Emigre* 19. **1991.**

Designed by Rudy VanderLans.

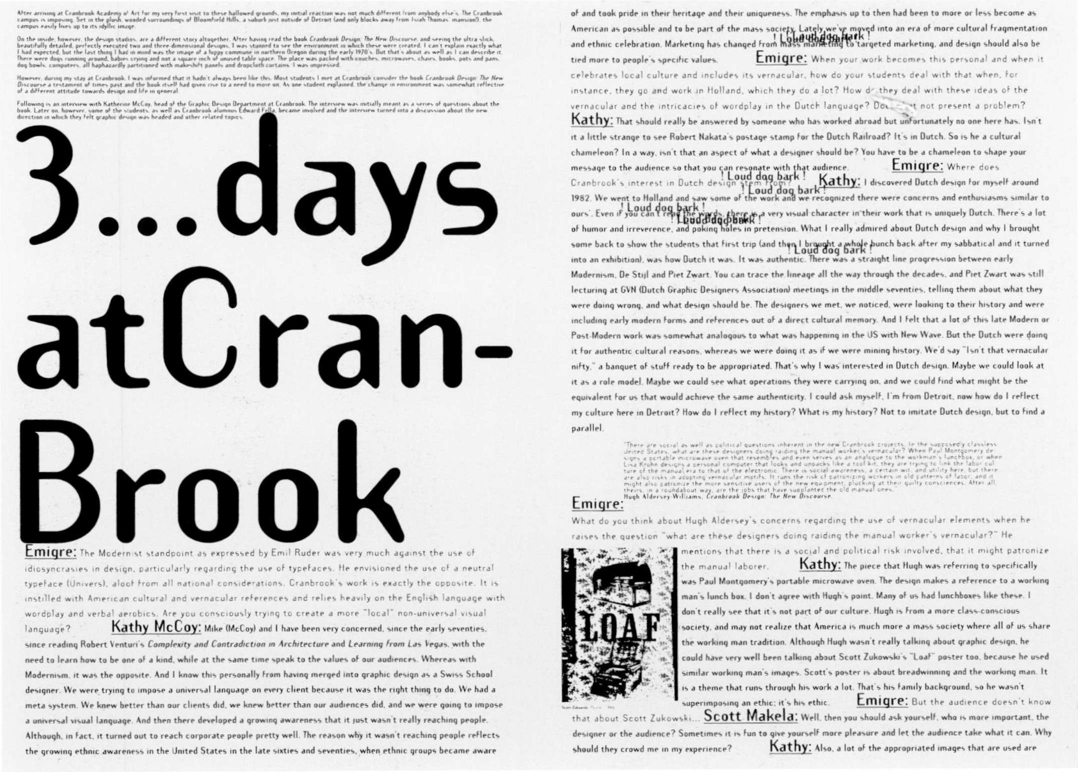

3...days atCran- Brook

Emigre: The Modernist standpoint as expressed by Emil Ruder was very much against the use of idiosyncrasies in design, particularly regarding the use of typefaces. He envisioned the use of a neutral typeface, Universal, aloof from all national considerations. Cranbrook's work is exactly the opposite. It is instilled with American cultural and vernacular references and relies heavily on the English language with wordplay and verbal aerobics. Are you consciously trying to create a more "local" non-universal visual language?

Kathy McCoy: Mike (McCoy) and I have been very concerned, since the early seventies, since reading Robert Venturi's *Complexity and Contradiction in Architecture and Learning from Las Vegas*, with the need to learn how to be one of a kind, while at the same time speak to the values of our audiences. Whereas with Modernism, it was the opposite. And I know this personally from having merged into graphic design as a Swiss School designer. We were trying to impose a universal language on every client because it was the right thing to do. We had a meta-system. We knew better than our clients did, we knew better than our audiences did, and we were trying to impose a universal visual language. And then there developed a growing awareness that it just wasn't really reaching people. Although, in fact, it turned out to reach corporate people pretty well. The reason why it just reaching people reflects the growing ethnic awareness in the United States in the late sixties and seventies, when ethnic groups became aware

of and took pride in their heritage and their uniqueness. The emphasis up to then had been to make American design as accessible and to be part of the mass society. Lately we've moved into an era of more cultural fragmentation and ethnic celebration. Marketing has changed from mass marketing to targeted marketing, and design should also be tied more to people's specific identities.

Emigre: When your work becomes this personal and when it celebrates local culture and includes its vernacular, how do your students deal with that when, for instance, they go and work in Holland, which they do a lot? How do they deal with these ideas of the vernacular and the intricacies of wordplay in the Dutch language? Does that not present a problem?

Kathy: That should really be answered by someone who has worked abroad but unfortunately no one here has. Isn't it a little strange to see Robert Nakata's postage stamp for the Dutch Railroad? It's in Dutch. So is he a cultural chameleon? In a way, isn't that an aspect of what a designer should be? You have to be a chameleon to shape your message to the audience so that you can resonate with that audience. **Emigre:** Where does Cranbrook's interest in Dutch design stem from? **Kathy:** I discovered Dutch design for myself around 1982. We went to Holland and saw some of the work and we recognized there were concerns and references similar to ours. Even if you can't really put a finger on it, there's a visual character in their work that is uniquely Dutch. There's a lot of humor and irreverence, and poking holes in pretension. What I really admired about Dutch design and why I brought some back to show the students that first trip (and then I brought a whole punch back after my sabbatical and it turned into an exhibition) was how Dutch it was. It was authentic. There was a straight line progression between early Modernism, De Stijl and Piet Zwart. You can trace the lineage all the way through the decades, and Piet Zwart was still lecturing at GVN (Dutch Graphic Designers Association) meetings in the middle seventies, telling them about what they were doing wrong, and what design should be. The designers we met, we noticed, were looking to their history and were including early modern forms and references out of a direct cultural memory. And I felt that a lot of this late Modern or Post-Modern work was somewhat analogous to what was happening in the US with New Wave. But the Dutch were doing it for authentic cultural reasons, whereas we were doing it as if we were moving history. We'd say "Isn't that vernacular nifty," a banquet of stuff ready to be appropriated. That's why I was interested in Dutch design. Maybe we could look at it as a role model. Maybe we could see what operations they were carrying on, and we could find what might be the equivalent for us that would achieve the same authenticity. I could ask myself, I'm from Detroit, now how do I reflect my culture here in Detroit? How do I reflect my history? What is my history? Not to imitate Dutch design, but to find a parallel.

Emigre: What do you think about Hugh Aldersey's concerns regarding the use of vernacular elements when he raises the question "what are these designers doing raiding the manual worker's vernacular?" He mentions that there is a social and political risk involved, that it might patronize the manual laborer. **Kathy:** The piece that Hugh was referring to specifically was Paul Montgomery's portable microwave oven. The design makes a reference to a working man's lunch box. I don't agree with Hugh's point. Many of us had lunchboxes like these. I don't really see that it's not part of our culture. Hugh is from a more class-conscious society, and may not realize that America is much more a mass society where all of us share the working man tradition. Although Hugh wasn't really talking about graphic design, he could have very well been talking about Scott Zukowski's "Loaf" poster too, because he used similar working man's images. Scott's poster is about breadwinning and the working man. It's a theme that runs through his work a lot. That's his family background, so he wasn't superimposing an ethic; it's his ethic. **Emigre:** But the audience doesn't know that about Scott Zukowski. **Scott Makela:** Well, then you should ask yourself, who is more important, the designer or the audience? Sometimes it is fun to give yourself more pleasure and let the audience take what it can. Why should they crowd me in my experience? **Kathy:** Also, a lot of the appropriated images that are used are

Page spread, *Emigre* 19. **1991.**

Designed by Rudy VanderLans.

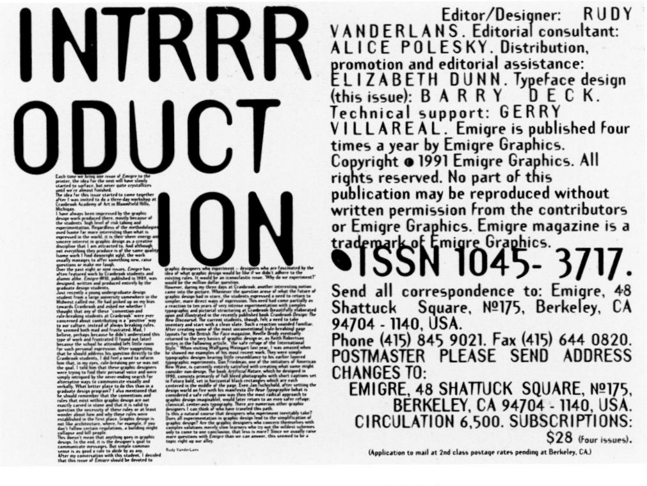

INTRRR ODUCT ION

Editor/Designer: RUDY VANDERLANS. Editorial consultant: ALICE POLESKY. Distribution, promotion and editorial assistance: ELIZABETH DUNN. Typeface design (this issue): BARRY DECK. Technical support: GERRY VILLAREAL. Emigre is published four times a year by Emigre Graphics. Copyright ● 1991 Emigre Graphics. All rights reserved. No part of this publication may be reproduced without written permission from the contributors or Emigre Graphics. Emigre magazine is a trademark of Emigre Graphics.

● ISSN 1045- 3717.

Send all correspondence to: Emigre, 48 Shattuck Square, №175, Berkeley, CA 94704 - 1140, USA. Phone (415) 845 9021. Fax (415) 644 0820. POSTMASTER PLEASE SEND ADDRESS CHANGES TO: EMIGRE, 48 SHATTUCK SQUARE, №175, BERKELEY, CA 94704 - 1140, USA. CIRCULATION 6,500. SUBSCRIPTIONS: $28 (four issues).

(Application to mail at 2nd class postage rates pending at Berkeley, CA.)

Page spread, *Emigre* 19. **1991.**

Designed by Rudy VanderLans.

Kurt Hobson (Sales/distribution), Berkeley office, 1991.

EMIGRE №19: Starting From Zero

Price: $2.95

Cover, *Emigre* 19. **1991.**

Designed by Rudy VanderLans.

In this issue *Emigre* asks the question "Does all experimentation in graphic design eventually lead to the simplification of graphic design?" In true modernist fashion, albeit loosely interpreted, the entire issue is set in one typeface, a sans serif (Template Gothic designed by Barry Deck), and all texts are set flush left, ragged right.

Emigre 20 featured interviews with expatriates Allen Hori and Robert Nakata. Respectively Canadian and American, both designers left their home countries to live and work as graphic designers in Holland.

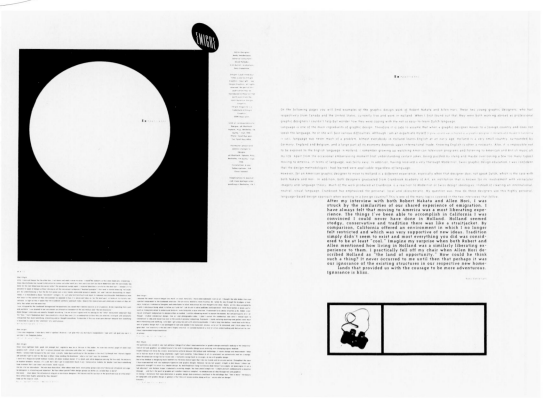

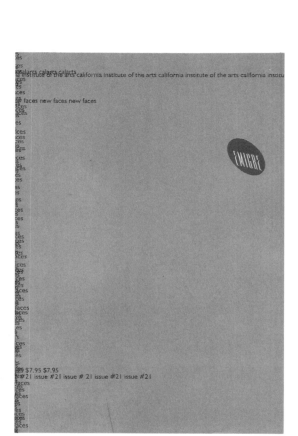

Cover. *Emigre 21.* **1992.**

Designed by Jennifer Azzarone.

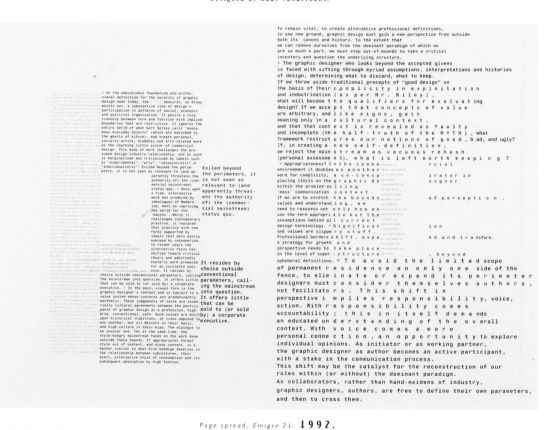

Page spread, *Emigre 21.* **1992.**

Designed by Anne Burdick.

Emigre 21 was produced entirely by the graduate and under-graduate design students at California Institute of Arts in Valencia, California. Edited by Jeffery Keedy, the issue consisted of actual school assignments whose mechanical parameters were slightly altered to fit the page size and printing restrictions of *Emigre.*

PAST
(in)tense /
future (im)
PERFECT

Page spread. *Emigre 21.* **1992.**

Designed by Christopher Vice.

Emigre: When did you start teaching at the London College of Printing?

Nick: In 1990. The college had kept in touch with me since I'd left, which they like to do with most former students. They approached me because they felt the students needed some teaching input from a younger designer of a different generation than most of the full-time staff there. I am one of about six younger part-timers, averaging one day per week each, at LCP. The current regime of full-time staff has been running the course for at least twenty years and are approaching retirement all at once. I feel that they are looking for a younger designer to stamp their authority on the course, which is something I'm not up to at the moment; especially not full-time. There is a big gap between us youngsters and the present set up — there will have to be some new full-time appointments of older designers to bridge that gap.

Emigre: Do the full-time staff determine how you should teach or are you given a free rein?

Nick: Fortunately, I'm allowed, and was from the beginning, encouraged to write my own briefs. When I started, it was just after the Berlin Wall had come down. The first brief I set was the **9'11" brief** that was very much inspired by what was happening at the time in Eastern Europe. I found myself putting a comparable amount of energy into creating problems for someone else to solve as I would put into solving them myself.

Emigre: I remember the briefs I had when I was in design school. They were a bit simpler.

9'11" Brief Something like: design a book cover for "War and Peace" by Dostoevsky. This is the nice.

you can see two colors, go to it. The briefs weren't unlike the briefs I now get as a professional designer. Why did you start writing such lengthy briefs?

Nick: Because I believe that strength of context is very important, and this takes time to build. I want the students to feel that with each brief they have an identifiable and well structured context within which to work; this I would find difficult to build if the briefs were shorter. The strong context cuts down the possibilities of interpretation that each student has to the brief, and makes sure that a superficial response to problem-solving is virtually ruled out; it isn't that important to give them technical limitations. I never say they can only use two colors, or do it at this size, because the limitations of a student lifestyle and that of government cutbacks in education will determine what they can afford to do anyway. I will give suggestions regarding the medium they might pick, whether it should take the form of a book, a poster, or an animation. I like to give them a scenario within which is a message that they need to convey and they must find their own forms and ways to do it.

Emigre: Why do you teach?

Nick: Because I enjoy teaching. At present, I feel that by constructing the complex problematic scenarios that are my briefs, and by watching and guiding students in their attempts at making sense of them, somehow in this idealistic setting, I am getting closer to identifying what the possibilities are: the possibilities of graphic design as a medium if all of us graphic designers were to truly realize what a great responsibility we have.

Emigre: How do you achieve that through teaching?

Nick: Most of the projects that I have set have close relationships to what is going on in the real world. Even though they are hypothetical, they are based on actual things that have recently happened, or are about to happen, or haven't happened but should happen. Maybe as a graphic designer you can influence social issues. I am trying to get the students interested in social issues and rescue graphics from the all-too-often superficial purpose of always producing, for its own sake, the cosmetic and the decorative.

Emigre: Do you feel you can have greater impact by influencing the students to think about such issues, than by being actively involved yourself?

Nick: Well, yes and no ... The point is that impact can be achieved *(continued on page 6)*

(continued on page 6)

Page spread. *Emigre* 22. **1992.**
Designed by Rudy VanderLans.

Devoted to Nick Bell, this issue focuses on the work and teaching methods of this young London-based graphic designer/educator.

Instant photo studio.
Sacramento office, 1992.

by a generation of designers all being actively involved, if, as I said before, we truly realise the great responsibility we have as graphic designers. My own impact so far has been dependent upon and limited to the opportunities that I've had in my own work up to now. I've touched little on social issues. It follows that our clients also must be made to realize that graphic design has a more socially responsible role to play than they first thought, but it is up to us to tell them.

Emigre: After reading the briefs and articles that you sent me, I was overwhelmed. The briefs are truly inspirational and thought-provoking. But at the same time, aren't you worried that the students are going to be quite disappointed and disillusioned once they finish school? Don't you fear that most students will eventually fall victim to the same frustrations as you did?

Nick: Yes, they will be disappointed. I was disappointed when I left college; that happens anyway. It is why at college we call the outside world the "real world," in anticipation of leaving our little ideal world. As a teacher, I am deliberately offering an alternative by producing briefs that contrast greatly to the ones they get all the other days of the week. It is a different perspective, a heightened one. Some of the students may have views on certain social issues, but maybe they don't believe that they could express these views through graphics. I simply try to point out there are ways to do this.

Emigre: After they graduate, what do you expect them to do with the things you teach them?

Nick: What I teach them is a small part beside that which they learn from all the other tutors on the course. I can understand your skepticism, and sometimes I worry whether I am just creating more problems for them. It sounds stupid, but just because there is no evidence out there of a market with an appetite for using socially conscious designers, this doesn't mean that I shouldn't provide the students with that working perspective. For 80 percent of the time, the students will be taught the skills to help them operate with ingenuity, as graphic designers have always operated over the past ten years or so, solving the same problems for the same sorts of client; there is nothing wrong with that. But the rest of the time, by doing one of my briefs, they will become skilled in ways of working for clients that aren't usually so lucky; e.g. the homeless. When they graduate, I would expect them to believe that as graphic designers they can achieve more through their discipline than is popularly told them through the example the "real world" gives them at the time they leave.

Emigre: But graphic design can't achieve much by itself. As a designer, you're always going...

(continued on page 2)

(continued on page 2)

This page is a door

Page spread. *Emigre* 22. **1992.**
Designed by Rudy VanderLans. Right hand page designed by Nick Bell.

Inside cover, *Emigre* 23. **1992.**
Designed by Rudy VanderLans.

Just as *Emigre* 15, this issue also introduced a number of typeface designs by various designers including Jonathan Barnbrook and Miles Newlyn. The feature article, written by Dutch type designer Gerard Unger, was about legibility, definitely a sacred area to some.

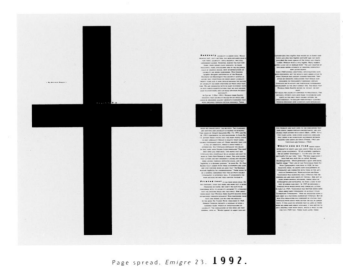

Page spread. *Emigre* 23. **1992.**
Designed by Rudy VanderLans.

1992 ( )

Continued

With *Emigre* magazine's circulation continually growing, and an ever-expanding number of designers using Emigre Fonts, VanderLans and Licko have not exactly decided to coast along. Besides her work on the design of new type-faces, Licko has taken on the increasing responsibility of streamlining the production, manufacturing, marketing, and distribution of the Emigre type foundry, now a considerable contender in the international type sales and distribution arena. With the same zest and inventiveness she applied to her typeface designs she now shares her knowledge on type creation with the young and upcoming type designers who license their fonts through Emigre.

VanderLans, having learned the hard way how to successfully publish and distribute an "independent" magazine, is now eagerly applying this acquired knowledge to helping his musician friends and other bands release and distribute their records. Emigre Music, the latest addition, releases "alternative" music on compact discs and cassettes.

These new ventures are evidence of Emigre's continued need to be involved with projects that challenge both their creative and business potentials. "THESE ARE SUCH UNIQUE TIMES," Emigre reflects. "MUSIC AND VIDEO ARE NOW GOING THROUGH THE SAME TYPE OF REVOLUTIONARY TECHNOLOGICAL CHANGES THAT GRAPHIC DESIGN HAS BEEN AFFECTED BY. WE HOPE TO BE INVOLVED IN THESE AREAS ONE WAY OR ANOTHER. ALTHOUGH WE OFTEN FEEL WE ARE STARTING FROM SCRATCH AGAIN, WE ENJOY EXPLORING THESE NEW CREATIVE AVENUES, AND ALSO ENJOY FINDING COMMERCIAL OUTLETS FOR THE RESULTS. WITH *EMIGRE* MAGAZINE WE HOPE TO BE ABLE TO CONTINUE DOCUMENTING OUR DISCOVERIES AND THOSE OF OUR CONTEMPORARIES."

Page spread. *Emigre* 24. **1992.**

Designed by Rudy VanderLans.

Page spread. *Emigre* 24. **1992.**

Designed by Anne Burdick.

First print ad announcing the Emigre Music label. **1992.**

Designed by Rudy VanderLans.

Page spread. *Emigre* 24. **1992.**

Designed by Rudy VanderLans. Photography (left) by Anne Burdick.

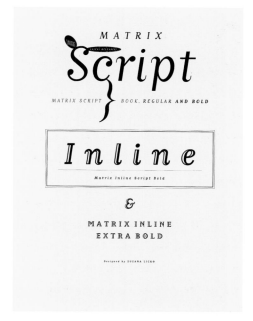

Print ad published in *HOW* magazine. **1992.**

Designed by **Rudy VanderLans.**

Print ad published in *Print* magazine. **1989.**

Designed by **Rudy VanderLans.**

Print ad published in *HOW* magazine. **1992.**

Designed by **Rudy VanderLans.**

Print ads Published in *HOW* magazine. **1991.**

Designed by **Rudy VanderLans.**

Print ad published in *HOW* magazine. **1992.**

Designed by **Rudy VanderLans.**

Survival

"It is a real struggle just to publish a magazine, let alone to maintain any kind of uniqueness. I've heard that every year there are approximately 400 new magazines started in the United States and only 2% will ever last beyond the first three years, which is also the average time it takes for a magazine to break even. Most magazines make money by selling advertising space. Since we never created a magazine for a specific audience, it was practically impossible to sell advertising. We had no demographics to show and a circulation of around 4,000 copies. Advertisers were difficult to find, and we soon gave up selling ads. Most of our income, therefore, came directly from sales of the magazine.

"We've certainly tried to get funding. But for one reason or another we have never received grants for EMIGRE magazine. We applied for an NEA grant twice and I once tried to get a grant from the Dutch government for EMIGRE 10. This issue was devoted to a cultural exchange project between graduate design students at Cranbrook Academy of Art and Dutch graphic designers. Unfortunately neither institution explained why the grants were denied.

Looking back, I don't regret not receiving that type of funding. EMIGRE has become profitable because, after five years, we have garnered a large enough group of sympathetic subscribers and outlets throughout the world who buy EMIGRE on a regular basis. We have been supported solely by sales of the magazine itself, and are proud of it.

"One of the major reasons why we have survived is because we decided to distribute the magazine ourselves, realizing that we could do no worse than most of our distributors. For a while we were entirely dependent upon a dozen or so small distributors for getting the magazine into bookstores and onto newsstands. We shipped hundreds of magazines all over the United States only to find out, years later, that with certain distributors large numbers of issues never even left their warehouses. Due to the standard "consignment" arrangements there was no real incentive for distributors or stores to sell magazines; unsold copies could always be returned to the publisher. Since it was too expensive to return a heavy magazine like EMIGRE, these unsold copies were usually destroyed. Subsequently there was a tremendous amount of copies wasted, which resulted in a significant financial loss. By setting up our own distribution we have taken on an enormous task, both in terms of administration and storage, but it has started to pay off, because now, every copy that we print is eventually sold. Stores have to buy C.O.D. and we don't accept returns. We give the stores a decent discount, and with a no-returns policy, the stores put in a little extra effort to sell the magazine, which is all EMIGRE needs. EMIGRE usually sells out within a few weeks.

"Of course, the Macintosh, too, contributed to making it financially possible for us to publish this magazine. Not only does it function as a great money and time saver in terms of typesetting, design, and production, but the Macintosh has also become an indispensable tool for all our administration, accounting, mailing lists, shipping data, financial projections etc., etc. We are true desktop publishers! Our equipment no longer fits onto one desktop, but the term 'desktop publishing' still seems appropriate."

(Rudy V.)

Emigre is now in a curious position, straddling opposite viewpoints. While still regarded as insignificant and downright detrimental to graphic design (underground, alternative, reactionary, rebellious) by some, others complain about the ubiquity of Emigre's typefaces (mainstream, establishment). Yet nothing elicits the Emigre team's response as when their work is being dismissed as yet another bland recycling of the formal aspects of Dadaist and/or Futurist design. They are quick to point out that "WE'RE THANKFUL NOT TO BE ABLE TO JUSTIFY OUR WORK IN AS GRAND A SCHEME AS A WORLD WAR AND RESULTING SOCIAL REFORM — THE BACKDROP THAT FUELED AND INFORMED THE WORK OF DADA. BUT WE DON'T BELIEVE THAT MAKES OUR WORK ANY LESS VALID. OURS IS A BATTLE FOUGHT AGAINST RAPIDLY CHANGING TECHNOLOGIES IN THE MIDST OF A GRAPHIC DESIGN 'INDUSTRY' THAT, SINCE THE DAYS OF DADA, HAS BECOME FIERCELY COMPETITIVE, IN A WORLD INUNDATED WITH VISUAL STIMULI. IF THERE IS ANY RESEMBLANCE TO THE WORK OF THE DADAISTS OR CONSTRUCTIVISTS OR FUTURISTS OR PIET ZWART OR WOLFGANG WEINGART, IT IS SIMPLY BECAUSE WE SHARE THE SAME CURIOSITY REGARDING THE UNLIMITED POSSIBILITIES OF TYPOGRAPHIC COMMUNICATION."

Sacramento office. 1992.

ARBITRARY Sans (Regular)

AaBbCcDdEeFfGgHhIiJjKkLlMmNnOoPpQ qRrSsTtUuVvWwXxYyZz

(1234567890)

PostScript typeface designs Arbitrary Sans Regular and
Arbitrary Sans Bold. **1992.**

Designed by Barry Deck.

ARBITRARY Sans (Bold)

AaBbCcDdEeFfGgHhIiJjKkLlMmNnOoPp QqRrSsTtUuVvWwXxYyZz

(1234567890)

Matrix Script

(Book) AaBbCcDdEeFfGg HhIiJjKkLlMmNnOoPpQqRrSsTtUuVvWwXxYyZz

(1234567890) *(Regular)* AaBbCcDdEeFfGg HhIiJjKkLlMm

NnOoPpQqRrSsTtUuVvWwXxYyZz(1234567890) *(Bold)* AaBbCcDdEeFfGg

HhIiJjKkLlMmNnOoPpQqRrSsTtUuVvWwXxYyZz(1234567890) *(Inline*

Script) AaBbCcDdEeFfGg HhIiJjKkLlMmNnOoPpQqRrSsTtUuVvWwXxYyZz

(1234567890) *(Inline Bold)* AaBbCcDdEeFfGg

HhIiJjKkLlMmNnOoPpQqRrSsTtUuVvWwXxYyZz(1234567890)

PostScript typeface designs Matrix Script Book, Regular, Bold, Inline and
Matrix Inline Bold. **1992.**

Designed by **Zuzana Licko.**

EXOCET (LIGHT)
ABCDEFGHIJKLMNOPQRST
UVWXYZ1234567890

EXOCET (HEAVY)
ABCDEFGHIJKLMNOPQRST
UVWXYZ1234567890

PostScript typeface designs Exocet Light and Exocet Heavy. **1992.**

Designed by **Jonathan Barnbrook.**

PostScript typeface designs Remedy Single and Remedy Double. **1992.**
Motion Light and Motion Bold. **1993.**

Designed by Frank Heine.

full color

roundup

Lori Jackson (sales),
Sacramento office, 1992.

MUSIC

EMIGRE

Compact Discs

(Music!)

Graphic design never sounded this good.

Promotional poster introducing the Emigre Music label. **1990.**

Designed by Rudy VanderLans.

Innocence at Will

Compact disc packaging. Stephen Sheehan, *Innocence at Will.* **1990.**

Designed by Rudy VanderLans.

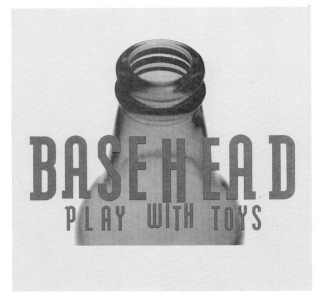

BASEHEAD
PLAY WITH TOYS

Compact disc packaging. Basehead, *Play With Toys.* **1991.**

Design and photography by Rudy VanderLans.

One word, two people.
Right on the heels of the critically
acclaimed debut album *Play With Toys* by
Basehead, Emigre is eager to introduce
Supercollider. This Los Angeles based band
consists of two members, guitarist/vocalist
Michael Horton and drummer Phillip Haut.
With only two people in the group,
Supercollider couples live guitar and
drums with sampled/sequenced sounds to
make up the crux of their music. And while
bands such as Joy Division/New Order,
Talking Heads and Sonic Youth have shaped
the group's sound, minimalist composers
(Steve Reich, Philip Glass) and artists
(Donald Judd, Ellsworth Kelly) are in a large
way responsible for Supercollider's unique
approach to alternative rock.
Catalog Number:
(Compact disc) Ecd 006, (Cassette) Ect 004.
Release date: August 30, 1991.
If you would like a promotional copy of
Supercollider, please give us a call
at **(415) 845-9021.**

Coming soon: **Fact TwentyTwo** - *The Biographic Humm*
Emigre, 48 Shattuck Square, #175, Berkeley, CA 94704-1140

EMIGRE

Postcard announcing new Emigre Music releases. **1991.**

Designed by Rudy VanderLans.

Emigre music sampler

no. 1

Compact disc packaging. *Emigre Music Sampler No. 1.* **1992.**

Designed by Rudy VanderLans.

MUSIC

Promotional poster, Stephen Sheehan, *Innocence at Will*. **1990.**

Designed by Rudy VanderLans.

Promotional poster, Every Good Boy, *Social Graces*. **1990.**

Designed by Barry Deck with Rudy VanderLans.

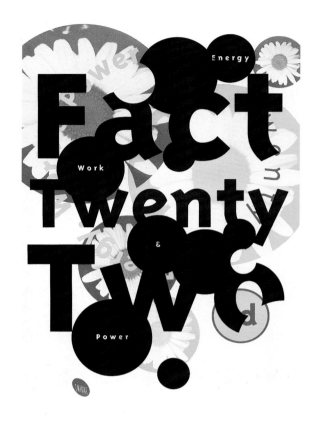

Promotional poster, Fact TwentyTwo, *Energy, Work & Power*. **1990.**

Designed by Rudy VanderLans with James Towning.

Promotional poster, Supercollider, *Supercollider*. **1991.**

Designed by Rudy VanderLans with Michael Horton.

Promotional poster, Basehead, *Play With Toys*. **1991.**

Design and photography by Rudy VanderLans.

MUSIC

"If Emigre (the record company) can do for pop music
what *Emigre* (the mag) has done for graphic design,
mainstream pop music just might sound (and look)
quite different in the not-too-distant future."
-Tower Records *Pulse Magazine*-

Introducing

Brand New Releases!

Fact TwentyTwo / Binary Race / Stephen Sheehan / Every Good Boy / Basehead / Ray Carmen

Bulk Rate
U.S. Postage
P A I D
Oakland, CA
Permit No. 1/29

Emigre

48 Shattuck Square, №175, Berkeley, CA 94704-1140

Flyer announcing new Emigre Music releases. **1991.**

Designed by Rudy VanderLans.

binary race

Promotional booklet. Binary Race. *Fits and Starts.* **1991.**

Designed by Rudy VanderLans.

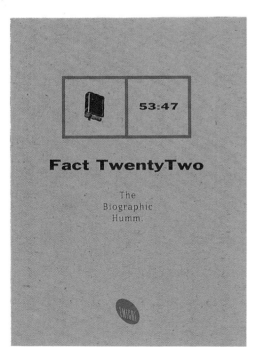

Postcard announcing the release of *The Biographic Humm*
by Fact TwentyTwo. **1991.**

Designed by Rudy VanderLans with James Towning.

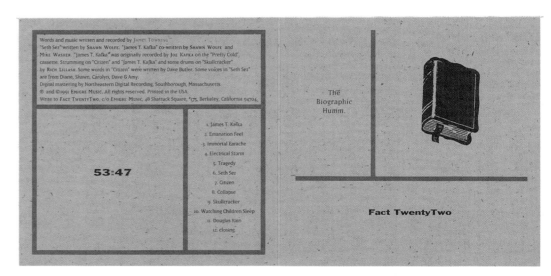

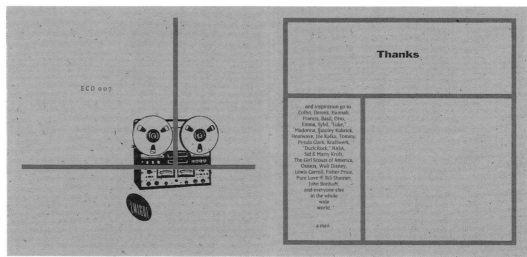

Compact disc packaging. Fact TwentyTwo. *The Biographic Humm.* **1991.**

Designed by Rudy VanderLans with James Towning.

MUSIC

All songs written and performed by Ray Carmen, except *Poor Reception* words by Craig Marks, music by *Mike Crooker*, and *You Just May Be The One* words and music by Michael Nesmith. All instruments and vocals by Ray Carmen, except backing vocals on *Brand New Boyfriend* by Ray Carmen and *Rob Crossley*. Produced and engineered by *Mike Crooker*. Recorded at Uneven Tracks Studios, Kent, Ohio. *Summer's Day* basic tracks and *Save My Soul* recorded at home. Mixed at Right Track Studios, Cleveland, Ohio. Remix engineer *Pete Tokar*. Editing by John Koschik. Digital mastering by Jonathan Wyner at Northeastern Digital Recording, Southborough, Massachusetts. Graphic design by Emigre Graphics.

ECD 008

Dedicated to my wife *Martha* and to my parents Jay and Ardith. (Mickey Dolenz does not play drums on this recording.)

Special thanks to Martha, Rudy at Emigre, Mike Crooker, GGE Records, Sean Carlin, Woodsy's Music, Pete Tokar, John Koschik, Bart Koster at Right Track, Rob Crossley, Clay Vause, Nick at *Spregg* and Mike Gonzalez. Also, Lawrence, Jim, Klaus, Mike Nesmith and my family. Extra special thanks to Douglas and Barbara Hura for Lasagna and legal advice. Photograph of Ray Carmen by Mike Crooker. Correspondence: POP! Productions, P.O. Box 167, Tatimadge, Ohio 44278-0167. This has been a POP! Production. All songs published by Radio Friendly (BMI), except *Poor Reception* published by Marks/Crooker, copyright control, and *You Just May Be The One* published by Screen Gems – EMI Music Inc. ℗ & © 1992 Emigre Music. All rights reserved. Printed in the USA.

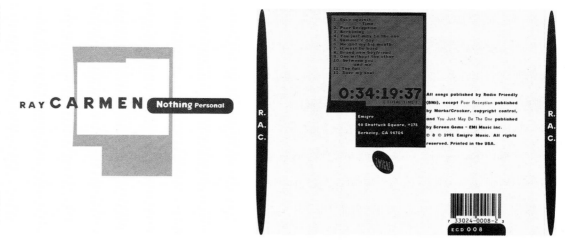

RAY **CARMEN** Nothing Personal

R.A.C.

Emigre
48 Shattuck Square, #175
Berkeley, CA 94704

All songs published by Radio Friendly (BMI), except *Poor Reception* published by Marks/Crooker, copyright control, and *You Just May Be The One* published by Screen Gems – EMI Music Inc. ℗ & © 1991 Emigre Music. All rights reserved. Printed in the USA.

R.A.C.

ECD 008

Compact disc packaging. Ray Carmen, *Nothing Personal*. **1992**.

Designed by Rudy VanderLans.

Wrapper designed to be wrapped around jewel box. Ray Carmen, *Nothing Personal*. **1992**.

Designed by Rudy VanderLans. Photography by Mike Crooker.

1. I'LL FIND YOU
2. JUDY CLIMBARROW
3. NEW TRICKS FOR OLD DOGS
4. FOR THE MEADOWLARK
5. GIMME MORE
6. FELL ASLEEP AT THREE
7. WILD
8. THREE DAYS IN A SPANISH RESTROOM
9. SIMMER DOWN

BALING WIRE AND BUBBLE GUM

AAD

Produced by Brian Deck and Erik Deerly with Brad Wood.
Engineered by Brian Deck and Brad Wood at Idful Music Corporation Chicago
℗ & © 1992 EMIGRE RECORDS
PRINTED IN USA
Emigre 48 Shattuck Square №175
Berkeley, California 94704

EVERY GOOD BOY

BRIAN DECK
DRUMS
ERIK DEERLY
VOCALS, GUITAR
GLENN GIRARD
GUITAR
DOUG MCCOMB
BASS

Lyrics inside!

ALL SONGS WRITTEN AND ARRANGED BY ERIK DEERLY WITH EVERY GOOD BOY, EXCEPT "FOR THE MEADOWLARK" WHICH WAS WRITTEN BY DEERLY/DEERLY AND "THREE DAYS IN A SPANISH RESTROOM" WHICH WAS WRITTEN BY DECK/DEERLY.

Produced by Brian Deck and Erik Deerly with Brad Wood.
Engineered by Brian Deck and Brad Wood at Idful Music Corporation Chicago

EVERY GOOD BOY the band

BALING WIRE AND BUBBLE GUM the album

Compact disc packaging. Every Good Boy, *Baling Wire and Bubblegum*. **1991**.

Design and photography by Barry Deck.

ADDITIONAL CREDITS
Carey Deadman: trumpet, tracks 6&8
Dan Halloran: tenor sax, 6
Dan Johnson: trombone, 6,8
Hexienny: "flat" vocals, 2,6
Dan Halvorsen: cello
Randy Henry: bass, 1,2
Rob Moore: guitar, 1,2

DESIGN: BARRY DECK
Engineered by Brian Deck and Brad Wood at Idful Music Corporation Chicago
ALL SONGS WRITTEN AND ARRANGED BY ERIK DEERLY WITH EVERY GOOD BOY, EXCEPT "FOR THE MEADOWLARK" WHICH WAS WRITTEN BY DEERLY/DEERLY AND "THREE DAYS IN A SPANISH RESTROOM" WHICH WAS WRITTEN BY DECK/DEERLY.
Produced by Brian Deck and Erik Deerly with Brad Wood.

EVERY GOOD BOY the band

BRIAN DECK
DRUMS
ERIK DEERLY
VOCALS, GUITAR, ALT & SAX
GLENN GIRARD
GUITAR
DOUG MCCOMB
BASS

BALING WIRE AND BUBBLE GUM the album

EVERY GOOD BOY BALING WIRE AND BUBBLE GUM

ECD 009
℗ & © 1992 EMIGRE RECORDS
PRINTED IN USA
Emigre 48 Shattuck Square №175
Berkeley, California 94704

Cassette tape packaging. Every Good Boy, *Baling Wire and Bubblegum*. **1991**.

Design and photography by Barry Deck.

MUSIC

audioafterbirth

Compact disc packaging. Audioafterbirth, *Commbine.* **1992.**

Designed by P. Scott Makela.

audioafterbirth

Wrapper designed to be wrapped around jewel box, Audioafterbirth, *Commbine.* **1992.**

Designed by P. Scott Makela.

Cassette tape packaging. Audioafterbirth, *Commbine.* **1992.**

Designed by P. Scott Makela.

MUSIC

BASEHEAD
BASEHEAD
PLAY WITH TOYS

Fact TwentyTwo

The Biographic Humm.

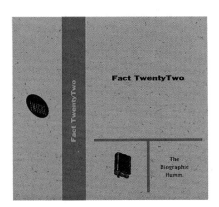

Honey Barbara

(feedlotloophole)

Contact:
P.O. Box 190105
San Antonio, TX 78280

Honey Barbara

(feedlotloophole)

ECD 012

Lyrics by
Ross Marlow

Graphic design by
Emigre Graphics.
Illustrations "sampled" from
the sketch books of
Edward Fella.

1. Big Black Berries
2. Mushroom
3. Bandwagon
4. Sun on fire
5. Two Birds
6. Down in San Antonio
7. We Don't Know
8. Pards
9. Desert Garden

ECD 012

Compact disc packaging, Honey Barbara, *FeedLotLoopHole.* **1993.**

Designed by Rudy VanderLans. Illustrations sampled from the sketchbooks of Edward Fella.

PROMOS

Poster announcing Frank Heine's Motion typeface. **1993.**

Designed by Elisabeth Charman.

PROMOS

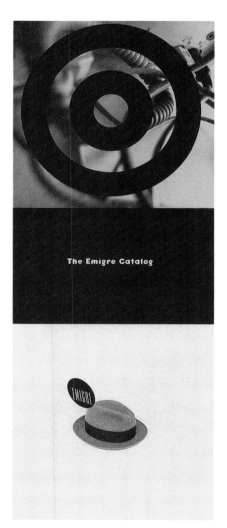

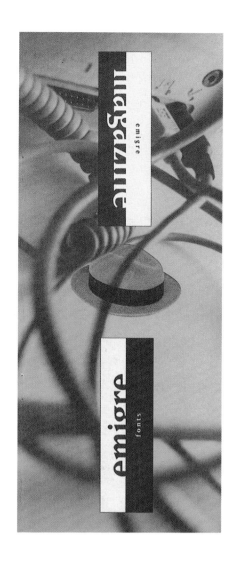

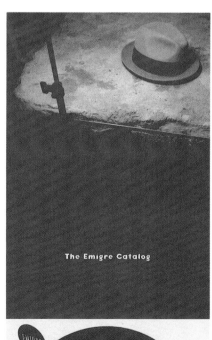

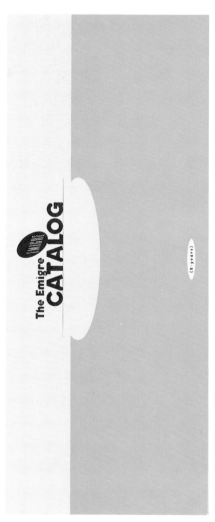

Emigre catalogs. 1990-1993.

Designed by Rudy VanderLans and Zuzana Licko.

PROMOS

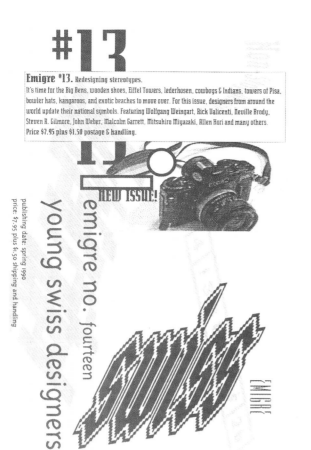

#13

Emigre #13. Redesigning stereotypes.
It's time for the Big Bens, wooden shoes, Eiffel Towers, lederhosen, cowboys & Indians, towers of Pisa, bowler hats, kangaroos, and exotic beaches to move over. For this issue, designers from around the world update their national symbols. Featuring Wolfgang Weingart, Rick Valicenti, Neville Brody, Steven R. Gilmore, John Weber, Malcolm Garrett, Mitsuhiro Miyazaki, Allen Hori and many others. Price $2.95 plus $1.50 postage & handling.

NEW ISSUE!

emigre no. fourteen

young swiss designers

publishing date: spring 1990
price $7.95 plus $1.50 shipping and handling

Flyer announcing the publication of *Emigre 14*. **1990.**

Designed by Rudy VanderLans

New Issue, Emigre #18

Type-Site

PIERRE DI SCIULLO (PARIS)
Phil Baines (LONDON)
ERIK VAN BLOKLAND &
JUST VAN ROSSUM (THE HAGUE)

Madam X (LOS ANGELES)

Price:
$7.95
(plus $1.50 shipping and handling)

Flyer announcing the publication of *Emigre 18*. **1991.**

Designed by Rudy VanderLans

Sacramento, CA 95819

№25

THE NEW ISSUE

mad
e
in ho
lland

$28

Flyer announcing the publication of *Emigre 25*. **1992.**

Designed by Rudy VanderLans with Anne Burdick.

zero left

Subscription renewal postcard. **1991.**

Design and photography by Rudy VanderLans

Price $5.00

EMIGRE

Publisher
Senior Editor

The Magazine That Ignores Boundaries
Published by Marc Susan and Rudy VanderLans

Postcard announcing publication *Emigre 2*. **1985.**

Design and illustration by Rudy VanderLans

Subscribe!

Non-Stop Design

Flyer announcing the publication of *Emigre 12*. **1989.**

Designed by Rudy VanderLans

EMIGRE
Graphic Design
SPECIAL

Flyer announcing the publication of *Emigre 10*. **1988.**

Designed by Rudy VanderLans

PROMOS

RUDY VANDERLANS (EMIGRE GRAPHICS)

NON-STOP DESIGN

WEDNESDAY, FEBRUARY 7, 1990

CLUB OF ODD VOLUMES, 77 MT. VERNON STREET, BOSTON

SOCIAL HOUR: 5:30 P.M.

DINNER: 6:30 P.M.

PLEASE RESPOND TO THE SECRETARY,

MELISSA CLEMENCE AT

(508) 879-2960 EXT. 4643

DINNER RESERVATIONS NOT HONORED WILL BE INVOICED AT THE

CURRENT RATE.

THE SOCIETY OF PRINTERS

FOR THE STUDY AND ADVANCEMENT OF THE ART OF PRINTING

OFFICERS:

SAMUEL ELLENPORT, *PRESIDENT*

JAMES R. GILL, *VICE PRESIDENT*

MELISSA CLEMENCE, *SECRETARY*

MARSHALL HENRICHS, *TREASURER*

COPENHAVER CUMPSTON, *AUDITOR*

COUNCIL:

JEAN EVANS

DAVID FORD

AL GOWAN

JOHN KRISTENSEN

Flyer announcing a lecture by VanderLans at the Society of Printers in Boston. **1990.**

Design and photography by Rudy VanderLans.

Music

Cover, Emigre Music Catalog. **1992.**

Design and photography by Rudy VanderLans

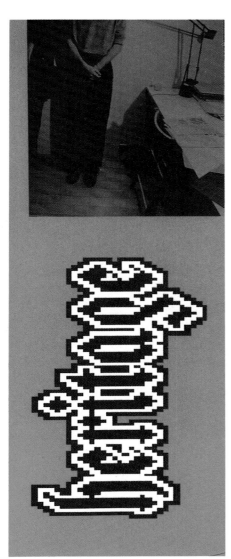

Flyer announcing the publication of *Emigre* 14. **1990.**

Design and photography by Rudy VanderLans.

EMIGRÉ

Non-Stop Design

Promotional poster *Emigre* magazine. **1989.**

Designed by Rudy VanderLans.

Poster for the exhibition *The Lion Rampant* for Artspace gallery. **1988.**

Designed by Rudy VanderLans.

Poster for the *Sculpture Grant Award* Exhibition for Artspace gallery. **1988.**

Designed by Rudy VanderLans.

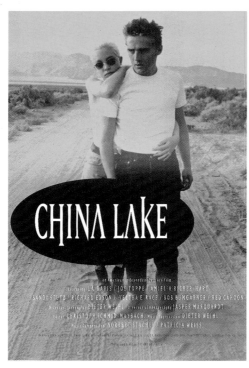

Poster for the film *China Lake* for Cairo Cinemafilms, San Francisco. **1987.**

Designed by Rudy VanderLans. Photography by Jasper Marquardt.

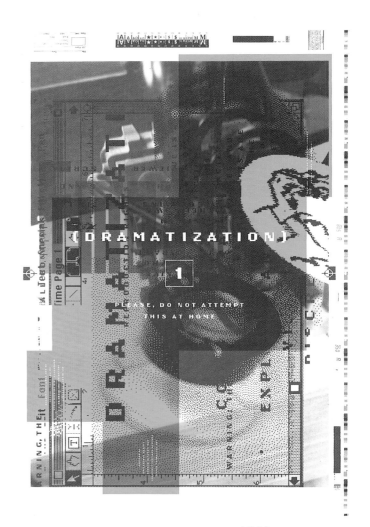

Poster/8-page signature, *Emigre 12*. **1989.**

Design and photography by Rudy VanderLans.

C O V E R S

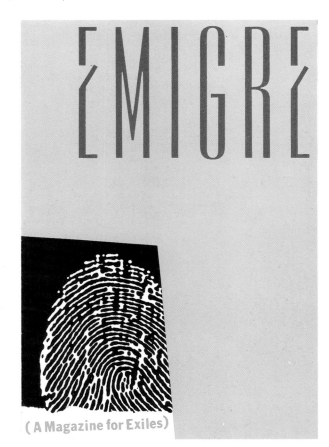

Cover, *Emigre* 1. **1984.**

Design by Rudy VanderLans.

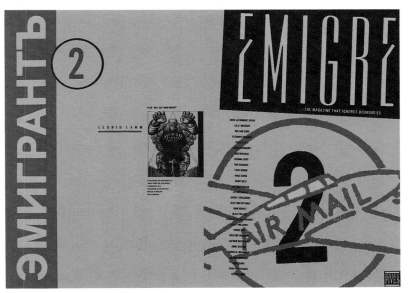

Back and front cover, *Emigre* 2. **1985.**

Designed by Rudy VanderLans.

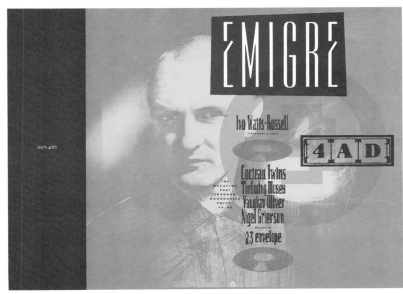

Back and front cover, *Emigre* 9 ("4AD" issue). **1988.**

Designed by Rudy VanderLans. Photography by Nigel Grierson.

Cover, *Emigre* 14 ("Heritage" issue). **1990.**

Designed by Rudy VanderLans.

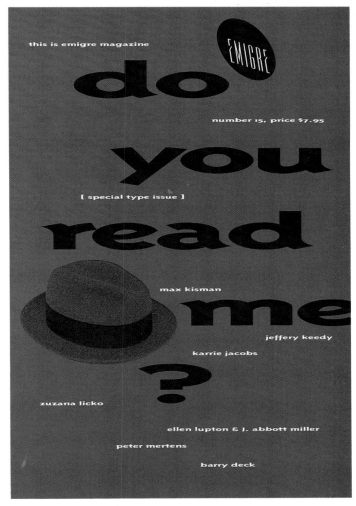

Cover, *Emigre* 15 ("Do You Read Me" issue). **1990.**

Designed by Rudy VanderLans.

COVERS

Cover, *Emigre* 20 ("Ex-patriates" issue). **1991.**

Design and photography by Rudy VanderLans.

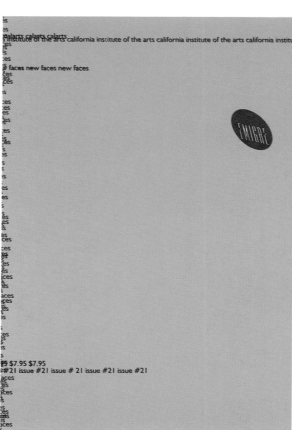

Cover, *Emigre* 21 ("CalArts" issue). **1992.**

Designed by Jennifer Azzarone.

Cover, *Emigre* 22 ("Nick Bell" issue). **1992.**

Design by Rudy VanderLans. Photography by Andy Rumball

Front cover. *Emigre* 23 ("Culprits" issue). **1992.**

Designed by Rudy VanderLans.

Back and front cover, *Emigre* 12 ("Press Time!" issue). **1989.**

Designed by Allen Hori, Warren Lehrer, Phil Zimmerman and Rudy VanderLan

Back and front cover, *Emigre* 13 ("Redesigning Stereotypes" issue). **1989.**

Designed by Rudy VanderLans. Back cover fax (Left) by Tibor Kalman.

COVERS

Cover, *Emigre 24* ("Neomania" issue). **1992.**

Design and photography by Rudy VanderLans.

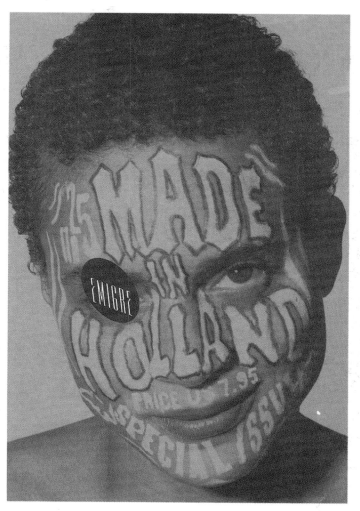

Cover, *Emigre 25* ("Made in Holland" issue). **1993.**

Design and photography by Armand Mevis.

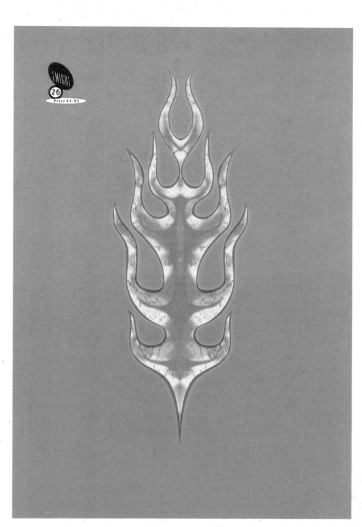

Front cover, *Emigre 26* ("All Fired Up" issue). **1993.**

Designed by Rick Valicenti and Tony Klassen (Thirst).

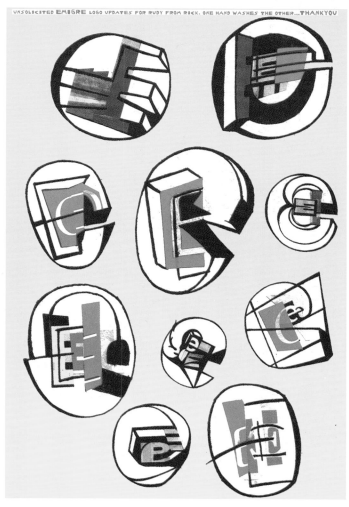

Back cover, *Emigre 26.* **1993.**

Designed by Rick Valicenti (Thirst).

Cnt-nd

Emigre's work has been published in the following magazines and books.

MAGAZINES

Design Quarterly, *Three New Faces* by Laurie Haycock Makela, Winter, 1993.
I.D., *The I.D. Forty,* January/February, 1993
Eye (England), *Reputations,* interview with Rudy VanderLans by Julia Thrift, No. 7, Vol 2, 1992.
Print, *Kicking up a Little Dust* by Michael Dooley, September/October, 1992.
Designers' Workshop (Japan), *Type-Image,* 1992, 1992, Vol. 9 N0. 56.
Confetti, *Fonts on the Fringe* by Poppy Evans, March/April, 1992.
Communication Arts, *Emigre* by Patrick Coyne, March/April 1992.
Nikkei Design (Japan), *DTP.* Nº10, October, 1991.
Communication et Langages (France), *Emigre, Les Nouveaux Primitifs Du Graphic Design,* Nº89, 1991.
Tategumi Yokogumi (Japan), *Desk Talking Point,* Nº33, Summer, 1991.
U&lc, *New Types, New Faces,* Volume 18, Nº2, Summer, 1991.
HOW, *Font Pirates: A Personal View,* 1991.
Print, *A Brave New World: Understanding Deconstruction* by Chuck Byrne and Martha White, November/December, 1990.
Step-By-Step, *Deconstructing Typography* by Philip Meggs, "Designers Guide," 1990.
Evolution (Japan), *Emigre.* July, 1990.
Blueprint (England), *New Directions in Products and Graphics* by Rick Poynor, Nº63, January, 1990.
Metropolis, *Say It Ain't So Joe* by Karrie Jacobs, January/February, 1990.
Baseline (England), *Emigre* by Mike Daines, "Bradbury Thompson" issue, 1990.
Design (England), *Two Colours, One Vision* by Mike Jones, August, 1990.
Ipso Facto, *Brave New (Mac) World* by Amy Fischel, 1990.
Print, *The 1980s: Postmodern, Postmerger, Postscript* by J. Abbott Miller, November/December, 1989.
Axis (Japan), *Design Works,* 1989.
How, *Emigre Art,* 1989.
Adweek, *Hot Shots,* 1989.
Blad (Holland), *From California With Love* by Gerard and Marjan Unger, Nº6, October, 1988.
Language Technology (Holland), *High Fashion Type,* 1988.
Design (England), *US Design,* 1988.
Publish, *Bold Faces,* 1988.
TYP (Holland), *Review,* NºB, April, 1988.
ID, *Culture Tabs,* 1987.
Design Week (England), *Surf's Up,* November, 1987.

BOOKS

20th Century Type (England) by Lewis Blackwell, Laurence King Publishing, 1992.
Designers on Mac (Japan) by Takenobu Igarashi, Graphic-sha, 1992.
Typography Now: The New Wave (England) by Rick Poynor, Booth-Clibborn Editions, 1992.
A History of Graphic Design (Second Edition) by Philip B. Meggs, Van Nostrand Reinhold, 1992.
Modern Magazine Design by William Owen, Rizzoli, 1991.
Graphic Design in America: A visual Language History, Walker Art Center / Abrams, 1990.
Low Budget, High Quality by Steven Heller and Anne Fink, WatsonGuptil, 1990.
Click by J. Ellen Gerken, North Light Books, 1990.
Experimental Typography by Kimberly Elam, Rizzoli, 1990.
New Americam Design by Hugh Aldersey-Williams, Rizzoli, 1988.
Pacific Wave: California Graphic Design (Italy), Magnus, 1987.

Tim Starback (Sales & Distribution) and
John Kessler (Technical crew), Sacramento
office, 1993.